Archie P. McDonald

A LIFE IN TEXAS HISTORY

EDITED BY
DAN K. UTLEY

TEXAS A&M UNIVERSITY PRESS
COLLEGE STATION

First edition

This paper meets the requirements of ANSI/NISO Z39.48–1992 (Permanence of Paper).
Binding materials have been chosen for durability.
Manufactured in the United States of America

Library of Congress Cataloging-in-Publication Data

Names: McDonald, Archie P., author, interviewee. | Utley, Dan K., editor, interviewer.
Title: Archie P. McDonald : a life in Texas history / edited by Dan K. Utley.
Description: First edition. | College Station : Texas A&M University Press, [2016] | Includes bibliographical references and index.
Identifiers: LCCN 2016010459| ISBN 9781623494612 (pbk. : alk. paper) | ISBN 9781623494629 (ebook)
Subjects: LCSH: McDonald, Archie P. | Historians—Texas, East—Biography. | Texas, East—Biography. | LCGFT: Oral histories.
Classification: LCC F391.4.M23 A3 2016 | DDC 976.4/1407202—dc23 LC record available at http://lccn.loc.gov/2016010459

Royalties from this book will be donated to the Archie P. McDonald Scholarship in History

Archie P. McDonald

DEDICATED TO

Judy McDonald, the love of Archie's life.
His story is hers, too.

Contents

Foreword

Many times I have uttered the phrase, "I knew *of* Archie McDonald before I *knew* Archie McDonald." I first met Archie in 2002, and although he did not remember it, I certainly did. I was a graduate student at Texas Tech University and he had traveled to Lubbock to attend the West Texas Historical Association meeting. I introduced myself and we engaged in a quick conversation about the upcoming East Texas Historical Association fall meeting, which I would attend, and that was the end of the conversation. It would be almost four years before we would have another chance to visit, although then it would be as fellow colleagues.

I accepted a position at Stephen F. Austin State University as an assistant professor in the spring of 2006, and my wife, Leslie, and I moved to Nacogdoches in August of that year. The whirl of the first year at a new job, coupled with Archie's busy schedule at the association—something I would learn about in the near future—meant that we would not be able to see or speak to each other that often, just occasionally at faculty meetings, passing each other in the hall, or waving in the parking garage. He did try to make sure I was involved in the association; he invited me to a board meeting and prodded me about taking a larger role. However, I was too consumed with trying to become a new assistant professor to take him up on his offers, and after my first year at SFA, in a sense I still did not *know* Archie.

That would change quickly. History department chair Troy Davis called me on a Sunday in the summer of 2007. His voice had a degree of anxiety when he said, "I really need to talk to you about something." He went on to say that Archie would be retiring from his departmental position in a year, which also meant that he would have to leave as the director and editor of the association. Dr. Davis said, "We really need you to agree to assume his position." I was not sure how to respond, but Dr. Davis asked me to speak with Archie before I made any decision.

I went to see Archie first thing Monday morning. The tension in the room was thick, and I sensed that Archie was leery of me, and I was certainly not sure I wanted to take on the added duties. The first words between us had some of that edginess, but as we began to talk I think we both realized we had more in common than we had previously thought. After well over an hour, we parted and I felt good enough about the situation that I told Dr. Davis I would take the offer of being the associate director for a year and then assume the full directorship in the fall of 2008.

I got to know Archie McDonald in that year. I began to come to his office every day, at first out of obligation and then because I enjoyed our time together. I discovered Archie was two different people: there was "Dr. Archie McDonald," the professor and executive director of the association. "Dr. McDonald" was formal, reticent, and yes, a little stuffy, although as I learned later, that was more an innate shyness than anything else. Then there was "Archie," and while that persona retained the former's grace, respectful air, and that particular strain of authority that some people have and some just do not, "Archie" was still different. He would laugh out loud at a good joke, throwing his head back as he guffawed and slapped his knee. He loved to talk about baseball, although not as much as he adored conversing about politics. The yellow dog in him could cuss Republicans with unconcealed contempt, but then I would watch him graciously find common ground at a Rotary meeting when we sat with a room full of Republicans. He was one of the most complete gentlemen I had ever met.

Archie became my mentor and counselor as I transitioned to the director's position. I sought his advice often, and when asked he gave it freely, although he never dispensed it without being asked. He stepped away and allowed me to make the position my own, and for that I will be eternally grateful. But most of all, Archie became my friend. He was the person I could go see when I needed not advice but just a friendly ear to bend. We could sit together and talk about things and then look up and realize that more than an hour, maybe two, had passed. I probably impeded his production more times than I realized, but he never let me know. Today, more than three years after his passing, I still miss him.

Through a series of oral histories conducted over several months, Dan Utley has ably captured both of those men I knew. As you read you will meet "Dr. Archie McDonald," and you will also get to know "Archie." The East Texas Historical Association owes much of its vitality and viability to Archie P. McDonald. Part of him remains within the association today, and it always will. That is as it should be.

M. Scott Sosebee
Stephen F. Austin State University
Executive Director, East Texas Historical Association

Acknowledgments

While my name appears in this book as editor, the reality is that I am only one member of a team that worked to preserve the stories of a remarkable man who served his beloved Texas at an interesting time in its history. He not only helped save history, he made a bit of it on his own along the way. The team within our team—the core of this project—comprised Archie McDonald and Judy McDonald. Their abiding love for each other, clearly evident throughout this book, was also in play as we started the project, and it remained a guiding force each step of the way. In a sense, each person is a book, but this is his, and it is also hers. Words cannot adequately reflect how much Judy's support and encouragement meant to this project and to each person who was involved.

The second-tier team consisted of Portia Gordon and Scott Sosebee, both of whom are mentioned in more detail later in the introduction. They also helped keep the project on course through encouragement and insights but also by fact-checking and clearing obstacles along the path to publication. Scott, in particular, is worthy of note for his diplomacy and perseverance in that regard. But beyond Portia and Scott there were others who played integral roles in the development of the book. First and foremost are individuals who, while serving as directors of the East Texas Historical Association (ETHA) in the course of this project, made important decisions about such matters as transcribing costs and archival needs. Not once was there a dissenting vote along the way; to their credit, each director and officer was fully on board from the beginning.

Thanks are also due the general membership of ETHA, people who, perhaps unknowingly, provided the type of friendship and vitality that kept

Archie McDonald at the helm of the organization for so long. It was work for him, no doubt, but he loved every minute of it, which shows in the words and stories he used to shape his memories. While not every name made it into the text, it is clear that the collective stories that encompassed so many are an integral part of the narrative. Many have noted through the years that ETHA was a reflection of Archie McDonald, but the converse is true as well—the organization helped define the character of the man as he became a renowned historian, an acclaimed public speaker, and a revered associational leader, as well as an unquestioned dean of Texas history. In that respect, he pushed the boundaries of East Texas all the way to New Mexico and Oklahoma, well across the South—and far beyond.

And finally, it is important to note the good work of Texas A&M University Press. Editor-in-chief Dr. Mary Lenn Dixon provided the initial encouragement for the project to go forward and recognized that the reach of this story was much bigger than just one region of the state. Timing, such a critical component of publishing, proved also to be a factor in her work on the project, as she decided to start a new chapter for herself with a well-deserved retirement. Fortunately, her replacement, Dr. Jay Dew, proved to be a worthy successor, one who became a friend and a valued team member as well. Even while transitioning back to his home state of Texas from Oklahoma, he learned of the Archie McDonald project and gave it his full endorsement. Raised in deep East Texas, Jay understood the immediate regional significance of the story, but as a historian he also greatly appreciated the broader context of what that story—the life of Mr. East Texas—has meant to so many others where the pines don't grow. Thanks, Jay, for reminding us, regularly and steadily, that we would get to this point in a timely fashion. And so we did.

Introduction

I first began attending meetings of the East Texas Historical Association (ETHA) in the early 1980s. I was a new and rather "green" historian who knew only a few people in the organization, or in the field of history for that matter. Almost immediately, though, I felt welcomed thanks to three individuals who are mentioned often in these pages: Max Lale of Marshall, Bob Bowman of Lufkin, and Archie McDonald of Nacogdoches. In those days, they were true presences in the organization, and I often remember them—with others—holding court in the lobby of the Fredonia Hotel as the ETHA fall conferences got under way. To me, who had a lot to learn not only about Texas history but also about the history of the region where I was born, sitting around and listening to the likes of these three was great entertainment. I always looked forward to returning to Nacogdoches and the various locales of the spring meetings to hear their stories.

As the years passed, I had the opportunity to know Archie better through his projects and commissioner service with the Texas Historical Commission, where I worked. He was always witty, supportive, fair, charming, and insightful. He could also be irascible and cantankerous, but in the good sense of a true Texas character. I grew to appreciate the depth of his integrity, both personally and professionally. As the ETHA director, he was a comfortable leader who ran meetings with purpose, humor, and brevity. He never dawdled. He set realistic goals and then built the networks to get them accomplished in the most efficient and practical ways possible. As a result, when I served as a board member and later as an officer, I came to appreciate the fact that we simply got things done the way he directed them, and the organization moved steadily ahead in programs, services, publications, and membership. Archie had a lot of friends who helped him with his organizational vision, and I was privileged to become one of them.

A few years back at a board meeting in Waco, I remember that as Archie gave some background on a few of the names associated with honors in our organization—Ralph W. Steen, C. K. Chamberlain, and folks like that—I realized that there was another generation of members for whom those names had no historical association. So, after the board meeting, as Archie and I walked along a hotel corridor together, I asked whether he had ever sat down with anyone for an oral history interview about his role in ETHA. To my surprise, he said no. At that point, then, we set out on a course that has resulted over a number of years in this publication. It is much more than it might seem at first. It is, at one level, an organizational history, a record of well-meaning people who have come together for decades to talk about and celebrate a region's rich past. But the other layers—and there are many—speak about community, family, respect, honor, friendship, and the fundamental aspect of history: change over time. There is the change that reflects new perspectives, new friends, and new leaders. But in a broader sense there is also the change in how a region interprets its past. All of these represent different journeys, but with capable direction like that provided by Archie McDonald, the braided paths moved ever forward.

Not long after the Waco conversation, Archie McDonald, Scott Sosebee, and I met at an Italian restaurant in College Station—the approximate halfway point between my home and theirs—and talked not only of oral history but also about where those collected memories might lead us. We all concluded it should result in a book, and I distinctly remember Archie saying, "Well, if we're going to do that, I have only one request: I want it to be through Texas A&M University Press." What followed was a conversation with our mutual friend, Dr. Mary Lenn Dixon, then an editor at the press. With her enthusiastically on board, the interviews began.

I interviewed Archie six times in his office on the campus of Stephen F. Austin State University, and each time it was like attending the best graduate history seminar I could imagine. He had a great memory, wrapped up in unique perspectives, and he seasoned it all with humor. There was laughter; lots of laughter. When all was said and recorded, we passed the digital files along to Archie's trusted friend and colleague Portia Gordon to help compile the transcripts and fill in any missing information misfiled in the memory banks over time. I am certain hers was not an easy task, although I know she enjoyed the interviews as much as Archie and I did.

When the writing began, it proved to be a bit more complex than either Archie or I had anticipated, because taking an interview structure and removing one of the voices, being careful to close up the resulting gaps in a narrative fashion and then connect all the remaining bits and pieces, simply takes time. And then, sadly, it was all interrupted by the limiting realities of a well-spent life. All too quickly Archie was gone, and the thought of continuing on that trail alone seemed daunting. But, as it turned out, those uncertainties quickly faded as Judy McDonald, Portia Gordon, and Scott Sosebee unselfishly joined up as walking companions. The finished product, then, represents the words of a great and caring man—a man who made a tremendous difference in Texas history and so many other ways—all preserved for the future by a group that loved him dearly. It is our hope that because of this effort, even generations who never knew Archie will come to appreciate his many contributions on their behalf. After all, he worked diligently throughout his life to preserve the past in the present for the future. For others, this might be a homecoming of sorts or another chance to sit and reminisce through shared memories with a friend and mentor. Regardless of what brought you to these pages, the stories are here—you'll just need to provide your own lobby space to appreciate them fully.

—Dan K. Utley
Texas State University

Archie P. McDonald

CHAPTER 1

It Is What It Is

A question I am often asked is, "What is East Texas?" I get that in terms of both the general concept and in the territorial boundaries, if any. Obviously, the East Texas Historical Association has no boundaries for membership; we have members in Germany and other countries, for example. But what is our sort of staked-out territory?

A professor at Texas A&M, Allan Ashcraft, wrote a great article about "What is East Texas?" shortly after our association came into being, and he had equal difficulty with the definition. It is what it is, is about the best thing I can say. But the way I operated when I was directing the association was first recognizing that the Sabine River on our east, the Gulf of Mexico to the south, and the Red River to the north obviously gave us some sort of definition. Beyond that, it has to be an imaginary line on the west, but I generally accepted the Trinity River. The Trinity River starts obviously in the Dallas area in the north, and there's a fork that goes very close to Fort Worth, and we have had some very good members from Fort Worth. If you follow the river south, it's angling to the southeast all the time, so I guess I deviate a little bit there and go over to Interstate 45 at least and say anything that's more or less within that boundary is East Texas. But we've had great meetings and great members from Texas A&M University, which is a little bit west of that. So it's got to be pretty nebulous on that.

Pine trees obviously are a defining influence, particularly in the eastern part of our region, because they run all the way from the Gulf of Mexico up to the Red River, but going west they run out about Crockett, discounting so-called Lost Pines over near Bastrop. The area I have just defined, though, is in reality the extent of the southern forest. One of the things that I learned from Dr. Walter Prescott Webb so long ago when he came down to teach a seminar at Rice was about the Great Plains and the three major landforms that converge in Texas. One of those, the southern forest, goes, with the exception of the interruption of the Mississippi Delta, all the way from the Atlantic Ocean to Crockett, Texas, approximately, to a line running north of that to a degree, and then after that you're on the plains. So that obviously is an aspect of East Texas. I don't think anybody really imagines East Texas without some timber on it, even if you are talking about the coastal savanna, where you have relatively small scrub vegetation all the way up to the Red River. You are getting trees, and that is one of the defining elements of the culture and the biology and the geography of East Texas.

I am kind of in the same quandary that a lot of people have been in when they ask the question, is East Texas the beginning of the West or the end of the Old South? I think obviously it is both. No matter where you go in what I have just defined all the way to Interstate 45, you will find the good and the bad of the Old South represented just as much as it is in the Old South, and I mean to say the good and the bad there, because we have both. But on the other hand, if you go to a restaurant in Nacogdoches, you're just as likely to see as many people wearing cowboy boots as wearing slippers on their feet, and they will have those ubiquitous hats on their heads. Evidently someone passed a law some time ago that says you must wear black felt in all seasons, at all times of the year, even at the table. But you know, there is a strong cowboy influence here, and there is some western influence here as well. I have used an expression in class sometimes, when I have hastily explained about the nature of our union as both federal and state—I say it is a political hermaphrodite. In other words, it is both at the same time, and I have been comfortable with that as a definition for East Texas.

I grew up in East Texas in the town of Beaumont. The East Texas of my youth probably would start with Hardin County. In other words, in Beaumont we regarded ourselves as coastal, and because of the French/Cajun influence we had as much Louisiana impact in our culture. For example, we ate rice with gravy and we ate a lot of seafood, but we were always conscious of being Texans, and somehow or other that seemed superior to Louisiana. It was a judgmental thing, you know; we're a little bit superior to those people over there. My wife, Judy, and I were talking the other day and noted that when we see cars in town with a lot of mud on them, we say that person lives on a dirt road. Well, in my youth we said they came from Louisiana, because Louisiana didn't have as many paved roads as Texas did, and that was often in fact a telltale sign. Now, Louisiana roads are as magnificent as ours, maybe a little better—but anyway, that's the way we felt.

Back then, if we mentioned East Texas, we were thinking of our relatives who lived in Burkeville in Newton County, for example, because Uncle Bill worked in the sawmill there. He actually worked in several, at places such as Wiergate, Birdville, Jasper, and Bon Wier. He was a planer operator and deaf as a post because of working around all that machinery all his life. One hand had two fingers missing, again a great testimony to having been employed in the mills. So that was East Texas to us, that is, pine trees. It is thicket country, you know. It is yaupon stuff—"tight eye" country it is called sometimes down in Hardin County, tight eye meaning you can't really see through it very far because the undergrowth is so thick. That was more East Texas to us. Lord a mercy, Nacogdoches and Lufkin were Oklahoma as far as we were concerned in those days.

From Beaumont, you just had to go a short distance up Highways 96 or 69 on the way to Kirbyville or Silsbee, and you were in our sense of East Texas before you got to either one of them. The topography had changed and was still relatively flat that far south, but the soil texture and the woodland growth were all different by then. In fact, it is still that way in north Beaumont. If you get past Parkdale Mall in Beaumont, yes, you are solidly in East Texas.

Studying a distinct region such as East Texas is relevant in our state because we are a composite of regions. Referencing Webb again, he taught that the three major landforms of the North American continent—the eastern forest, central plains, and western mountain basin desert country—all converge in Texas. We are not the only state that has some aspects of those, though I think we are the only one that has a whole lot of all three of them, and so it is crucial to understanding Texas. It is important to sort out the difference between the east and the west or what we call South Texas or the Panhandle, because we have been confused about those things before. The University of North Texas in Denton is located a good deal south of West Texas State University, now West Texas A&M University, and Southwest Texas, now Texas State University, is in Central Texas, so our concept of geography as we have applied it even to our educational institutions is based on our cultural concept of regions.

Texans have grappled with this geographic distinction, and it is important to us. There is maybe not as much friendly rivalry between East and West Texans as between Longhorns and Aggies, but we are tending that way; we have always tended that way. But that is a fraternal rivalry that is in-house stuff. That is when you might have a knockdown drag-out fight with your brother, but then somebody else comes along and it is the two of you against them. So we are all conscious of being Texans first and foremost, and being eminently proud of that fact.

But then we are also proud of the region we represent. An old friend of mine from "over there," Max Sherman, was running for attorney general—and I wish he had been elected. Regardless, his wife, Sarah Alice, came over campaigning for him with a friend, and they drove from Crockett to Nacogdoches and spent the night with us. They commented that as they drove Highway 21 between these two destinations, which is for the last forty-five miles heavily timbered, they just thought those trees were going to get out in the road with them, because they had come from Amarillo, where you have to hunt a long time for a tree and you have to water it when you find it. So, they were intimidated by the fact they could not see the sky; it is closing and claustrophobic, you see. But when I go out to West Texas, I am not intimidated, and I am certainly impressed by that huge vista that I can see. You know, you can see a lightning storm dozens of miles away, it seems, and golly that's a lot different than when it has to come up over the trees before you see it. My point, though, is that we are Texans; we are that first and always. My mother-in-law, may she rest in peace, when she and my father-in-law would travel out of state and stay in a motel, she would always make up her bed in the morning because, she said, "They know we're from Texas."

There's no question in my mind that by studying a region we learn more about Texas history in general. Although there is a strong Spanish heritage in South Texas, for example, the earliest Spanish activity within Texas, other than the *entradas*, was the attempt to put Mission San Francisco de los Tejas over here as a signpost to the French—which didn't work very well, but it was an attempt to keep them from coming into Spanish-claimed territory, and that was of course in response to the coastal explorations of La Salle.

Then later on, the Spanish do the mission experiment again, that time the result of Saint Denis's movement into Texas. But San Antonio doesn't come along until 1718, and then it's just the mission. There was not going to be a town there for a long time after that. There were early settlements along the Rio Grande, but the river was no boundary at that time. The purpose of El Camino Real is to get here to what is now East Texas. Terán de los Ríos blazed the trail in 1691 to get to about twenty-five miles from where we are now. Over the years, though, the Hispanic cultural influence and population/occupation were very heavy in the South Texas area up to at least San Antonio, but not beyond that. As a result, East Texas developed an Anglo-American and African American regional history. We also have to give Native Americans their part of the story, and later on Swedes, Wends, Germans, and others.

With regard to the formation of the East Texas Historical Association, geography definitely played a role. Lee Lawrence, of Tyler, one of the four founders of the modern incarnation of the association, remarked that one of the motivating factors for organizing was that the first members wanted an association of like-minded people. They could not always go to the Texas State Historical Association meetings, though. I think Lee did, but he met lots of other people who maybe didn't have the leisure or the wherewithal to make those trips and spend three or four nights in a hotel in Austin; they always met in Austin in those days. The organizers just wanted more, I guess, than that one annual meeting, too.

Now there was an association before the one we now enjoy, which dates to 1962. In 1929, the first faculty member at Stephen F. Austin State University was employed just to teach history. The founding president of the college, Alton Wilton Birdwell, had been a social studies teacher at Southwest Texas State Teachers College in San Marcos. He had a Peabody degree, but he was at Southwest Texas when the legislature finally authorized appropriations for the establishment of SFA for East Texas in the 1920s. It was specifically designated for East Texas. The first guy who was actually hired to teach history here was George Crocket, who was the Episcopal rector here and in San Augustine, and the author of that monumental *Two Centuries of East Texas*, which despite its title is really the history of the San Augustine area up until Crocket's birth. Much like Henry Adams, I guess he didn't think anything important happened after he was born. But in any event, he was hired as a history teacher here because it was his love, and he was the one who organized the first East Texas Historical Association.

I think Crocket's motivation was largely self-study. He undoubtedly had a good general theological education, which prepared him to study almost anything that he wanted to. He apparently had the same drive for *association* with people of like mind, so he issued invitations to the initial meeting in 1929, here in Nacogdoches. He and Dr. Birdwell both presented historical talks. Dr. Eugene Barker was also one of the early program presenters. He was a distinguished historian at the University of Texas in Austin—a formal kind of man who was one of the main gurus of the Texas State Historical Association. He and a couple of other guys were its patrons—I should say patron saints, really—for the first couple of decades. There was probably no more prestigious name in Texas history in 1929 than Eugene Barker. After that, they gathered the papers and published them in a bulletin, they called it, and it came out under the title of the college that hosted the gathering that year. So, in 1931, for example, there was the *Bulletin of the East Texas State Teachers College*, Commerce. I don't have all the early copies, but I have a few thanks to Ralph Goodwin. Ralph came down to a meeting shortly after I took over, and he brought a whole box of these things. They were just lying around up there in their History Department, I guess for forty or more years. He wanted to get rid of them so he brought them to us.

In the early days, the association was viable, but limited. I'm sure it comprised mostly history teachers, maybe a few laity, but probably not so much. It was just big enough to have $300 in assets. The reason I say that is that shortly after I became director, the widow of Dr. Charles Chamberlain brought me three $100 bonds that the association had left when it went out of business. Chamberlain took over sometime after World War II when he replaced Fletcher Garner as chairman of the History Department at SFA. The bonds probably came to him through Fletcher Garner, who was the chairman of the social studies in the History Department from early on and all through those years. That was the original East Texas Historical Association, and it went out of business as a casualty of the Depression. The bulletins date from 1928 to 1931. I have no record of anything after that that I've ever been able to find, but it would be interesting to know if somebody does have in an attic or trunk somewhere a later *Bulletin* or membership list, or anything of that nature, because we never did have that over in our office. The organization likely folded because leadership was lacking. Leadership is always the key in every endeavor as far as I'm concerned.

In the 1960s, though, there was change in that regard. The two real founders of the association then were F. Lee Lawrence, a Tyler attorney, and Francis Ingraham Tucker, an attorney in Nacogdoches. Both had a strong interest in history. Like many in the organization, their interest went back many years, and I shared that passion with them. I knew I wanted to be in history in one way or another after I took Bob Warren's history class at French High School in Beaumont. By the way, I later had the great pleasure of writing a letter of recommendation for Bob when he wanted to go back and get his doctorate, and that was a neat kind of payback moment. He was my inspiration in history. Apparently Lee and F. I., although lawyers, had that same drive for history all along, but what they lacked was the institutional machinery. That's when they engaged Ralph Wright Steen.

It was the academics that headed the first organization, but it was a mix of academics and lay historians that proved to be the important ingredient in the second East Texas Historical Association. It was also a hallmark of my directorship and my editing of the *Journal*. The laity had to have representation. I can tell stories about the lengths I sometimes went to ensure that, to put it shortly here, they pay most of the bills, frankly because that's most of the membership and they deserve representation. In any event, Lawrence and Tucker lacked the institutional machinery to accomplish their goal, so they engaged SFA through Dr. Ralph Steen, who was the president. He came here in 1958 and retired in 1976, and in most ways he is the father of the modern university. He brought it from about 2,100 students to nearly 12,000 students before he retired.

I want to spend a little time talking about these important founders of the association. Lee Lawrence was a native East Texan, and his father was a lawyer. Lee studied law as well and was also prominent in local history groups in Tyler. He was the father of the Camp Ford Historical Association and very influential in the Smith County Historical Society, which I judge is, or at least at one time was, one of the most active county history societies in Texas. He was on the council of the Texas State Historical Association (TSHA) when I went on the council, and he was president three or four years before I served in that office. In other words, he was just a history-minded fellow all the way. He was generous, too. He and his wife, Ann, called me aside one day and said, "What would you do with a certain sum of money if we gave it to you?" I said, well, I'd start a publication series, so that's how the Ann and Lee Lawrence Monograph Series began, and it remains an active program today. Not only did Lee give me that sum of money to work with, he supplemented it, and since his death, Ann has supplemented it when necessary. Now it is set up on a revolving basis so that it has far more money in the fund than they gave, because we have had two or three of those publications which were really good sellers, especially Fred Tarpley's *Jefferson: East Texas Metropolis* and Bob Glover's *Camp Ford, CSA*, which was based on a book he and Lee had done earlier. Lee also did all the legal work for getting our charter, pro bono of course.

F. I. Tucker lived on East Austin Street in Nacogdoches in a little white brick bungalow which I always thought was far too small for such a big personality. He was kind of the conscience of history keeping here in Nacogdoches, far beyond any of the history teachers either at the university or secondary levels. He was the guy you sought out to find out who was related to whom, two generations, three generations back, and where something was located then. It was from him that I got a copy of the 1841 map of Nacogdoches that I published later on in the *Journal*, and it showed literally every structure that was in the town at that time, and that was about thirty or forty, and they were all right along what is now East Main Street in the downtown area.

Tucker was also a native East Texan, although his family came from Georgia. He was a proud Nacogdochian and a very prominent attorney. I don't know how to measure prominence with wealth and that sort of thing, but he was sort of the "go to" lawyer for the old-timers. When we moved here in 1964, he was a very well-respected and well-thought-of man. He had an interesting sister. Her name was Elizabeth and she had been at LSU some years before I was there. She knew T. Harry Williams, who was my major professor, and she apparently just absolutely loved him. Now I don't necessarily mean that in an erotic sense, despite what I'm about to tell. Harry was a bachelor when she knew him, and one of his first books was a groundbreaking work on the American Civil War called *Lincoln and His Generals*. He signed her copy of the book on the flyleaf "To Elizabeth with lust and passion, Harry." I confess I borrowed that—didn't say plagiarized, because I always changed the name, but I borrowed that a number of times with very good friends who I thought would find it funny.

Elizabeth Tucker was a dear lady and important, by the way, to our story. She and one of the other retired history teachers, a woman named Lois Blount, ran Boynton Library's East Texas Room, which was admittedly more museum than archives. It was over in the building that now houses the computer center for the campus. The East Texas Room housed the archives, and they were the first people as far as I know who ran that. We now have a first-rate archives, of course, which grew from that early effort. Miss Tucker and Miss Blount were always sort of patron saints for me, those two plus another librarian named Willie Earl Tindall, who graciously helped a young historian. If I went to the library they would help me look for anything, and doubtless they granted me privileges that were not ordinary, like being able to take some materials to my office and work, and that sort of thing.

Dr. Steen was born in Clyde, out near Abilene, and he was a graduate of the University of Texas. He taught history and then became chairman at Texas A&M, where he was the author of the textbook called *Texas: Our Heritage*, which came out in 1962 and influenced generations of Texas historians and teachers. Steen left the history chairmanship at College Station to become president at SFA. He promised the Board of Regents, which oversaw several colleges, that if he worked real hard he thought he could grow the enrollment to 3,000 by 1970; it turned out to be 10,000 by then. We caught the wave of a lot of people going to school in the sixties, and we grew by 1,500 to 2,000 students a year, so they were hiring warm bodies around here, which is how I got a job. They were hiring just about anybody who wanted to come here, you know, and I wanted to come back to Texas from Kentucky, so we made a good marriage on that.

Steen had to overcome a lot of community resentment, for he inherited to a degree a situation in which his two predecessors had worked hard at being important members of the local community. Both were members of prominent churches, Sunday school teachers, Rotarians—they were involved. Then there was the fact that his immediate predecessor died literally in office. He had a heart attack in 1956, and when Dr. Steen showed up there was immense sympathy for Dr. Boynton's widow. She had just occupied the new presidential mansion and didn't want to get out of it. She had designed it, and it was to be her house—and then all of a sudden it was not going to be. Steen sort of forced the issue because he had a family that he needed to move in and was living in a motel as a university president. There was for a while some community resentment against him. But by the time he retired, he was the heart and soul of the Nacogdoches community and to a large degree of East Texas, because when the Deep East Texas Council of Governments created an award for leadership and service in the region, they made him the first honoree and then named the award for him.

Dr. Steen told me a funny story. He spoke all over the place but never used notes because, as a short man, he said his bifocals wouldn't focus on the podiums, which were usually too high. So he just learned to speak extemporaneously. So he's in Jasper at a Lions Club, I believe, and the head Lion of the state is there to install officers. When Steen went he thought he was going to be the keynote speaker. Come to find out, he's way down the list of speakers, and this governor, or whatever he was, installed all the new officers, and as each one would go up they would put a piece of a puzzle up on a board, and when it was all over the image was of a lion. So the guy is real proud, and he sat down and sort of mumbled to Steen, "You ever seen anything like that before?" Steen said, "Not since the third grade."

Steen didn't suffer fools very lightly. He said he did put up with me and we became good friends. He was an important man here, and ironically when he retired, everybody was scared to death he was going to leave town and the place would close up or something. He did leave for eighteen months; he went to Austin to work for the Higher Education Coordinating Board, but then he came back. He was a widower by then, so he came back here where his best friends in the world, Bill and Frances Turner, lived. Bill was the dean of fine arts here, and Steen brought him with him from A&M. Bill had directed the Aggie chorus, and he brought him over here to be the Music Department chairman. In any event, Steen came back here to live, and then when Bill Johnson became our president, it was like the reversal of roles. Ralph Steen is now the saint and Bill Johnson is the heel for moving Dr. Steen "out," even though he had already retired. Bill painted the shutters on the institutional manse blue instead of dark green like every southerner knows they are supposed to be. You would have thought original sin had been committed right here. Twelve years later when Bill left, the same community reaction happened all over again. I mean, you build your nest and everybody learns to love you, and then the next new guy has to do it all over again.

That brings me really back to C. K. Chamberlain. His name was Charles Kincheloe Chamberlain, but everybody called him Dick. He was principal of Nacogdoches High School; the original structure now houses an elementary school and is named the Chamberlain Building. He came to SFASU after World War II, and he did not have a doctorate, but there were a lot of people on the faculty then without doctorates. But he realized he needed one, so he went to the University of Texas and earned one, and later he became chairman of the History Department and thus my boss until he retired in 1970. He was also my predecessor as director of the association, although the position title was editor. So, he was the one who really set up the machinery for an association. As the department chairman, he had a secretary who could share duties with him. He had two prominent historians, Robert Sidney Maxwell and James Nichols, on faculty who took an interest in the work and really helped. Even more critical to the mix, though, was Tommie Jan Lowery, who became the secretary of the association and held that job well past the time when I took it over, as long as, she said, she could "handle it out of her purse." And then when we started having enough money to really have to keep close tabs on, she decided she didn't want that responsibility, and that's when we first started having the association's secretary also be the treasurer. We have not had one bad one in that position; all of them were honest and competent. We never had a minute's problem fiscally in the thirty-seven years I was involved intimately with the association's affairs. We also had good graduate students who helped. Joe White, a past president, was one assigned to the association work.

So anyway, the deal was that the people I've mentioned would organize the East Texas Historical Association, and it would be housed on this campus. Dr. Steen agreed to pay for the printing of the journal. From the beginning this was to be an SFA program, with an open invitation to anyone interested in membership. The plan was for the association to be sponsored by the university, and the staff would always be on this campus. In fact, it's a part of our constitution; the director has to be a full-time faculty member at Stephen F. Austin State University. Chamberlain would become the first editor. Now, editor in those days meant director, because he's the registrar of members; he received the money, which Tommie Jan took to the bank. He probably did the program chairman's job as well. He and the people he recruited from the History Department were the backbone of the labor to get the association going.

From the beginning, membership was open to all. They did not have to be history teachers. They could be undertakers or lawyers, as long as they had an interest in history. In fact, lay members have always constituted more than half of the total membership. As a result, I always made sure if I had any influence with the nominating committee that we alternated presidents. Now, sometimes what constitutes a lay historian and a professional historian may be sort of loosely interpreted. In a strict sense, history teachers would be considered the professionals, although some of the lay historians might be better researchers and writers. So we might have been a little loose like that sometimes, but I maintained that principle in the presidency and on the board, and I made certain that lay people got published, both for articles and reviews.

The organization of ETHA began with an invitation that went out from Dr. Chamberlain to all the history departments in all the institutions in East Texas, as well as to lay people known to have an interest in history. They were all invited to come to Nacogdoches one Saturday late in September 1962 to have an organizational meeting—not to read papers, but to have an organizational meeting. I think there were probably fifty to a hundred in attendance. There was a good representation, and I've heard from the founders they were very encouraged by that enthusiasm. It was an event waiting to happen, and that was the leadership that made it happen. They left the charter membership open for a year, so they originally had about four hundred charter members.

From the beginning, the members agreed to a two-meeting-per-year concept: spring and fall. They met in September to organize, and the first conference was the following spring in Jefferson. There they read the first papers ever presented at an ETHA meeting. Seth Walton of Marshall presided at the Excelsior House. Bob Glover of Tyler presented a paper entitled "Incident at Lynn Flat." Susan Miles of San Angelo spoke, and Allan Ashcraft talked on "East Texas in the Election of 1860 and the Secession Crisis." There was a luncheon for which the fee was $2.50 a person. F. Lee Lawrence was elected president and presided at the luncheon, where John Ben Shepperd of Gladewater, and later Odessa, was one of the presenters. Ruth Lester, of Jefferson, who became a well-known preservationist, was also active then. Then the next meeting was in October 1963 in Nacogdoches.

The two-meeting concept was important to the character of ETHA. Nacogdoches was the headquarters, so it was the site for the fall meetings, but the board also wanted to meet elsewhere in East Texas in the spring as an outreach. It ultimately worked, I think very well, particularly when we met on what you might call the peripheries of the region. For example, if we were meeting in Paris, a lot of the Southeast Texas people would not consider such a long trip, or conversely, when we had an early meeting in Saratoga at which Senator Ralph Yarborough was one of the principal speakers, because he loved that Big Thicket, well, Texarkana people had a similar concern about distance. But we show our flag in the various regions and we give on an alternating basis nearly everybody an opportunity to attend a meeting, present a paper, or just to come and listen. The one exception to this geographical rule is Galveston. We have put on four or five meetings in Galveston and in that case location did not matter—they came from Texarkana, they came from Denver, and elsewhere, to eat at Guido's, or something like that.

In general, the organization likely grew by word of mouth, because we were fortunate in having some key people in a lot of communities. For example, Lucille Terry took up the mantle in Jefferson from Ruth Lester. Mrs. Terry was a founder and a very prominent and active member of the board, and she was the kind of person who would have rounded up everybody in Marion County who had the slightest interest—maybe whether they had an interest or not. I've known a lot of people, in the early days particularly, who said, I'm a member because so and so made me. You know, give me your five dollars and you're a member now, and they would occasionally come to a meeting and some of them would stick.

In the early days of the organization, there were several communities that were particularly well represented. Certainly Jefferson, Marshall, and Nacogdoches fit into that category, but also San Augustine and, thanks to the work of Miss Eliza Bishop, her hometown of Crockett. A lot of the early membership depended on the work of individuals. In Beaumont there was Preston Williams, who, though he was a historian of France and chairman of the History Department at Lamar University, was always very supportive.

So were the people who gave papers and wrote articles, like Ralph Wooster and other members of the department. Preston Williams never missed a meeting as long as he was still running the department. In Marshall there were various people early on, but eventually it was Max Lale. He was the hammer that kept that county interest pretty much in line. We had a lot of people in Nacogdoches, and in those early days much more support from the secondary education teachers. Tyler, of course, had Lee Lawrence and Bob Glover, and later on Linda Cross and others. In San Augustine there have been several people through the years, but there's never been a dynamo like Willie Earl Tindall, so she would be the outstanding representative of that community bar none. We had some earlier on from Longview, like Ken Durham, who was very active there. Seth Walton with East Texas Baptist was very active, and Frank Jackson and Ralph Goodwin in Commerce were as well. We don't have anybody now from Commerce that I'm familiar with, but in the early days you know they were pretty active. There were so many who helped create the association and kept it moving forward in the 1960s, and many of them were strong ambassadors for East Texas. We owe them a debt of gratitude.

CHAPTER 2

A Personal Journey in an East Texas Context

Before I mention my entry onto the ETHA scene, it might be good to go back in time and pick up my East Texas credentials. My mother was Pernemia Cowan, who went by the name of Nem. Pernemia was actually her name, but everybody pronounced it Pernema—I don't know why—so somewhere along the way she became Nem. She married Archie McDonald (no middle name) after they both had migrated to Texas from Beauregard and Vernon Parishes in Louisiana. Their families were very different. My mother's father was a traveling man, I like to say, because it raises eyebrows, but he was a brakeman on the Cotton Belt Railroad, and her mother was the daughter of Frederick Craft, a farmer in Vernon Parish. My father's father was named Madison McDonald, and he was a very prominent businessman. In fact he listed himself unabashedly as a capitalist. His wife was Olivia Seaman, my grandmother. I like to say that both were refugees of the Depression, although they did this in the earliest part of the thirties. In fact, mother's family moved down first in the 1920s, and she was actually a 1929 graduate of Beaumont High School. She was a classmate of Babe Didrikson, later known as Zaharias. They only had eleven grades back then, by the way.

My folks' story was perhaps typical of the farm-to-city migration happening then, and Beaumont was probably the easiest city of promise for them to reach. Lake Charles wasn't that big then, and I don't think Shreveport was yet. Baton Rouge was a lot farther away. Beaumont was already a very active seaport and obviously an oil and gas headquarters, and a refining center. There was work there, they thought. My father was a barber by trade, and he later became a cattle commission agent. Let's get them married first so you won't think badly of my background. They met I think there in Beaumont, even though they came from adjacent parishes in Louisiana, and they married in Beaumont in 1931. They lived on Liberty Street in a middle-class residence less than a mile from Beaumont.

My father, I remember, could walk to the barbershop on notorious Crockett Street, where he worked. A man named Red Kelly owned the place, and he was very nice to me. When I would go in there I would always be treated very royally. Red Kelly had the back chair, which is where the owner always was; this was a five- or six-chair barbershop. My father had the next chair, which was the logical progression in the hierarchy, and the guy who had the front chair was a very good barber, a Cajun name Migues. The reason he was in front was because all the people who knew him would come in and patronize the barbershop. This is in the same block, but on the opposite side of the street from the infamous Dixie Hotel, by the way. The Dixie Hotel was in Beaumont's history, I guess, the most notorious whorehouse among several that were on that street. That was the street where the red-light district was permitted, tolerated, perhaps even encouraged by the local law enforcement, because it was at least compartmentalized. I guess they could agree that if they had to do any policing there, it could be easily done. The Dixie was where the famous madam Rita Ainsworth operated, but she was a little later in time than when my father was in a barbershop across the street. The hotel building is still there and is sort of a museum you can rent out for parties, dances, and wedding receptions and what have you. You still have to walk up those stairs to get up there to it, but it is still there. It is about the only thing that is left; there is a little entertainment district on Crockett now, but lots of the old buildings are gone, including the Texas Club, which is where I learned to shoot pool.

In any event, my father worked there, and mother, of course, stayed home as good ladies did in those days. At home meant a house occupied by the three of us plus mother's mother, mother's sister, and her mother's sister, too—Aunt Venie, Aunt Jonnie, Mama—which is what we all called my grandmother—my mother, my father, and me. We all lived in a five-room house with one bathroom, very common and ordinary in those days. There was one hall that, believe it or not, connected every one of those rooms. The bedrooms were probably ten feet by ten feet at most, but the kitchen may have been bit larger, because that tended to be the center of family life in those days.

I was the only child in the house for a while. My father died when I was eight years old. By the wartime my father was already incapacitated from tuberculosis, and he passed away on June 4, 1944. Eighteen months later, my mother remarried. Because of the way the months broke, I was ten at the time. She married a wonderful man named George Harvie Tucker, and they had three children. My stepfather was from Navarro County, where he grew up on a cotton farm near a little community called Corbett. By the 1940s, his sister was already in Southeast Texas, married to a man in the dairy business, and they lived in Beaumont then, but later on in Kirbyville. So my stepfather went to work at Kelly Dairy, too, until the war came along, and he went to work in the Pennsylvania Shipyard. In the meantime, Mother had gone to work at the telephone company as a telephone operator. That was long before dials and touch-tone, so she operated a switchboard and literally connected people by using lines to connect the circuit on the switchboard. She would go across the street to what was known as the Enterprise Café for breaks or even lunch if she didn't take her lunch. My stepfather was one of the men about town who would go around looking for girls in places like that. Then he found more than he bargained for, I imagine.

One of the yarns I've always enjoyed telling is that after the war when the shipyard job went away, he went back to the dairy and had the downtown business route for a while and I would go around with him on Saturdays. There were a lot of delivery trucks in those days—laundry, diapers, milk, ice—and the companies frequently hired young men to go with them to do the grunt work. We would go to various places where old girlfriends would be, and he would say, "This is my son." And their jaws would drop, because here's this young teenage kid standing in front of them, and they wondered where in the world I had been while they were dating him, but he never in my presence ever explained anything to anybody. I cannot tell you how much I appreciated that. He did not choose to explain me away as "my wife's kid"; I was his son.

There were probably several storytellers in my family, because when I was growing up there on Liberty Street in Beaumont we were often visited by relatives who were also Louisiana refugees, and they were forever talking about Uncle Jim and Aunt Florence up in Vernon Parish and that sort of thing. I appreciated family history, and I believe that was reflected in my schoolwork. My aptitude tests showed I was most suited for what they then called social studies, but they didn't say history point-blank in those days. That is the way I always was supposedly bent. But the person who I think influenced me the most was Florence Lee "Flossy" Heinrich, who was my seventh-grade Texas history teacher. This would have been in Gary or French Junior High—it went by both names—in Beaumont, and as her name might imply, she was somewhat Teutonic in the way she conducted the class. I won't say I was kind of the pet, but I was probably the most interested kid in the class, and so she naturally showered me with attention. I have done the same thing for fifty years. You find a student that is really interested and you teach to that student, and I guess that is what she did. She engaged me particularly in the Texas history part of it. In high school, the best teacher I had other than my English teacher was historian Bob Warren, and that is when I decided I wanted to be a history teacher. So, when I enrolled at Lamar College and they asked what I wanted to be, I said a history teacher, and they told me I needed to major in education. I had no reason to know any different, so I did, and two years later I was still taking all the required history stem work, much of it from a guy named Merrill Rippy. He later left and went to Ball State in Indiana. He taught from the Socratic method, and that really appealed to me. It was a question-and-answer kind of thing. In other words, he would give an exam based exclusively on reading. Then for the next three weeks we would discuss that material. This was supposed to be based on our reading and then we would discuss it, but discussion was him asking a series of questions. Then you would respond to those questions, and if you could not, he would go to the next person, but in those days we were not aware that shrugging the shoulders and saying we didn't know the answer were not acceptable, so we were all competitive. We wanted to be able to answer the question and we did not want it to pass on from us to someone else. That appealed to me and I responded to it very well, and I have fifteen hours of undergraduate instruction from Merrill Rippy. I also have three hours from Ralph Wooster on the American Civil War, and that was influential in that I became first a Civil War historian. So they were definitely influential, as was a man named Preston Williams, who taught virtually all the European history at Lamar in those days, and he was a good teacher, too.

Now, I've never regarded myself as being a fast reader; I am probably a pretty careful reader and I do tend to absorb that in which I'm interested pretty well, but I would not in those days. More than likely I would have had a ball of some kind in my hand back then rather than a book. The writer that I mostly read at the time was the western writer Will James, and I still have a lot of his titles in my library. He was a real cowboy and he wrote in what we called local color dialect. I also read John R. Tunis, who specialized in sports, as in *The Kid from Tomkinsville* and so forth.

I also loved watching movies, and I could do that every day. I was lucky to have some great theaters to attend in Beaumont. The Jefferson, with its magnificent chandeliers, always reminded me of the Phantom of the Opera. The Tivoli, which is where all the "shoot-'em-ups" came, was on Liberty Street, and on down the way was another theater called the Peoples, which was, by the way, the only integrated theater in town in those days in that African Americans were admitted to the balcony. That's what I mean by integration; they were not on the same floor as the white patrons. They had a separate entrance, too. I never attended it, but there was the Lamar out in the South Park area and later the Gaylynn Theater on Calder Avenue, which was kind of upscale for those days. There was also the Rio, which was also on Pearl Street with the Liberty Theater. But none of them ever matched the grandeur of the old Jefferson, which is still a magnificent edifice, recently restored. I went to the Organ Club there every Saturday morning. I was never bold enough to get involved in the juvenile talent show they had, but I'm ashamed to admit I made fun of kids who did. Regardless, we got in for nine cents or something like that and could watch that talent show, the bouncing ball sing-along, and four or five serials—shorts of various kinds. Most often there would be a shoot-'em-up and then a newsreel, which, particularly in those days, featured a lot of World War II news.

The cowboy stars of the time included Lash LaRue, Johnny Mack Brown, Tex Ritter, and Whip Wilson. They all had sidekicks like Smiley Burnette and Fuzzy Knight and Dub Taylor, who later went on to a very long career in A films. "Cannonball" was his sidekick name in those days, and he always played an irascible old guy. He probably made hundreds of films as many characters, but he was always Cannonball to me.

Anyway, I've had a lifelong interest in movies, although for me the really good moviemaking ended about thirty years ago. Every now and then a good one like *The King's Speech* will come along, but I like the old classics and I like the John Wayne version of what's proper on the screen. When profanity came in, a lot got lost to me. I have often said I have never learned a new word from the movies—I knew all those words and I knew when and how to use them, and probably did more than I should. But it always just seemed gratuitous to me. The most erotic scene I ever saw in a movie was in John Wayne's *The Cowboys.* There's a scene in there where he's old, and his wife is, too. He's going to take these cattle off with this bunch of little kids and the dialogue is "What can I bring you?" and she said a little pair of red shoes, which harks back to Red River—"a little pair of red shoes and you home again." And he said, "You don't want much," and she said, "I'll think of you when I go to bed," and he said, "You do and you won't sleep." And he gets on his horse and rides away.

Despite such distractions, I remained focused on my goal to be a high school teacher, at least through the first part of my undergraduate work. At Lamar, I had four good friends, three of whom became college teachers and one of whom became rich. The rich one was Elvis Mason, who was my debate partner, and he became a prominent investment banker in Dallas. The ones who became teachers were Leland Bellot, of Port Arthur, who served with distinction as a history professor and administrator at Cal State–Fullerton, and Charles Alexander, of China just outside Beaumont, who became a baseball historian at Ohio University. We were all in the same classes together because there were only two or three advanced history classes, and we were all competitive, but we also helped each other. When Leland got to Rice University, he said to me, "Why don't you go to graduate school, too?" I said, "Graduate school. What's that?" I really did not particularly know. I knew my professors had these advanced degrees, but coming from my background, it really did not seem like a possibility in those days. Besides, I was married to Judy by then. But Leland said, "Why don't you come to Rice with me?" So I wrote the school but did not get an immediate reply, because unbeknownst to me, all the assistantships had been given out.

One Saturday when we had nothing else to do, Judy and I drove over to Rice, which had residential colleges. The master of Hanson College was a guy named William Harris Masterson, who was in the History Department. He was later dean and for about five days interim president one time, but that is another story. Masterson was interesting. He was a western historian who lived there on the campus, so when I showed up at the front door and said I wanted to talk to someone about going to school there, the only person on campus they could refer me to was this guy who happened to be in the History Department. So I go over to his house on campus to tell him what I wanted, and apparently he liked me, because when I went home, within two weeks they contacted me to say there were no more history assistantships and the money was all gone. But there was an unused engineering scholarship, so if I wanted to come over for a year, I could, but there was no guarantee there would be a second year. The second year was crucial at Rice, because there was no summer school. No one could finish in a year, so it would take two years. My alternatives were teaching at Orange High School or China High School, and I would have made $2,700 if I had seven class preparations, took up tickets at the football game, and drove a school bus. I would be making less than half of that as a graduate assistant, but Judy helped make it a possibility by continuing to work. Together, our pay was meager, but we had a good life and those were great years.

Rice is where I met the noted military historian Frank Vandiver. He had already published *Mighty Stonewall* and of course *Confederate Blockade Running through Bermuda*, which got him started. At the time, he was the boy genius of the Civil War history world and had just come to Rice. Haskell Monroe was his one and only graduate student before I got there, but he soon added me, Nancy Head (later Bowen), and a guy from New Hampshire named Bill Taylor. Working with Frank was such a marvelous opportunity because he was so dynamic. He would call me up at midnight sometimes and tell me to go to the library and to have something on his desk by nine in the morning. He might not get there until after lunch, but I would make sure it was there when he asked for it. He would bring Judy and me over to his house to meet his wife and children. I had a very strict personal code in those days and did not drink. I was serious about it, but I was not a Baptist yet. I was a Christian Science church member in those days and very strict on alcohol. Frank just absolutely took delight in trying to make me take a drink, and one time I did take a little sip of something. It was absolutely horrible! I hated it and made a face, and he just thought that was the funniest thing in the world. But my greatest ally was his wife, Susan, because she would say to Frank, "Now remember how so-and-so treated you, so stop it." He would straighten up for about five minutes, but he loved to bedevil grads. He used to say, "Never give a graduate student an even break." That was his mantra, but nobody ever did more for me than he did, including ultimately getting my most successful book published. That was *Make Me a Map of the Valley*, about Stonewall Jackson's topographer, Jedediah Hotchkiss. That work started with Frank Vandiver. He protected me greatly through my time there. The History Department there at Rice had some schism in it, and I think he saw that if I stuck with him I was going to get caught in the vise, because there was a lot of jealousy of him. He was a popular historian at the time and had been interviewed by CBS and other organizations, so there was a lot of jealousy of him. So, he said, "I want you to go somewhere else for your PhD. I think it'll be good for you to have three different degrees." He tried to get me into Wisconsin, which was premier in those days, and I had started the Hotchkiss diary for my master's thesis—at least it was supposed to be my thesis. My Lord, the thing is volumes long and I was up to about four hundred pages and was just into 1862, so he said that would be more than enough for a thesis. But he encouraged me to finish the topic for a dissertation, because it was based on an important diary that few people knew. It was the document historian Douglas Southall Freeman used to redate the entire valley campaign of Stonewall Jackson, because Hotchkiss was with the general every day. Hotchkiss was the topographical engineer with the 2nd Corps of the Army of Northern Virginia. He had intimate close-quarters connection with Jackson, Lee, J. E. B. Stuart—all the main generals of the Confederate side of the war. My final work became kind of a little cult book when it was published in Virginia. It is in its fifth or sixth printing now by SMU Press.

There is an interesting perspective on how I came to use the diary. The Hotchkiss family gave it to Douglas Southall Freeman, and he alone had access in the 1930s, and he used it as a major source for *Lee's Lieutenants*. Then it stayed in Battle Abbey, the Virginia Historical Society headquarters building in Richmond, where nobody saw it until the family finally got tired of them not returning it, and they went and physically removed it. Then they sold it to the Library of Congress in 1946, along with Hotchkiss's other papers, most importantly his maps, because he was the topographer of the

Confederacy. Vandiver found it early in the 1950s when he was working on Stonewall, and it was an important source there and has been to many others, including Stonewall Jackson biographer James I. "Bud" Robertson. It remains a truly significant primary source of Civil War information.

Anyway, Vandiver wrote to Wisconsin but was not encouraged by the reply, so he called his good friend T. Harry Williams at LSU, and of course he paved the way and Harry said, "Yeah, come on." Williams arranged it for me to have an assistantship, and at LSU I was a grader the first year. The second year I was the chief grader for the American history sections, and the third year I had the one and only teaching assistantship they had. I had two classes of three hundred students, but I had a graduate-student grader, and I was also writing my dissertation. It was a fun time.

Harry Williams took me on and became the second really major influence in my professional career. I have said many times that those two guys—Vandiver and Williams—vaccinated me in that I was working under the guidance of the two most published and distinguished military historians in America in the 1950s and 1960s. That is what they did. I lectured for both of them while they were off speaking and serving as presidents of the Southern Historical Association. I was making indices for them, and I was doing all the things publishing historians do, under their supervision, and learning how to do it all well. That was just what I thought historians did, so when I got into the teaching side, I did all of that, too. That was just what you were supposed to do, and I was astonished to find that a lot of my colleagues didn't necessarily see it that way at all. They had altogether other ideas about what it was historians did.

Vandiver and Williams were great friends, but they could spar with the best of them. They teased unmercifully, but they would have died for each other. I remember that during the summers, since Rice had no summer school, Vandiver would go to Baton Rouge and teach a nine-week session. So he's over there and Williams called one night and Susie answered the phone. He said, "Let me speak to the world's second greatest Civil War historian. Quick as a flash, Susie replied, "Oh, you want Dr. T. Harry Williams," and she then gave him his own phone number. There is a long pregnant silence and then finally Harry said, "Goddamn it, Susie, let me talk to Frank." That's the kind of relationship I guess they had. It served me very well because, you know, he took care of me—"This is Frank's boy and he's going to be Harry's boy now, so take care of him." And Williams did. I still prize and cherish a comment he made on one of my book chapters. He scrawled it on the back of a calendar page. When I finished my dissertation, I was teaching at Murray State in Kentucky. Williams had a summer place in upper Wisconsin; I mean, you could see Canada from there. It was a cool place, much cooler than Baton Rouge and less humid, and he was up there while we were mailing the final rewrites of the dissertation chapters back and forth, and on that calendar page, writing about two or three months from where we were at the time, he jotted the note, "Good enough." That was the highest praise I had ever received.

When I was done, here is what happened. I sent it to LSU Press, because obviously I wrote it there and they were the premier publisher of Civil War material in 1965. The Civil War Centennial had just ended, so the director sent my manuscript back and said he could not publish it at the time since the market was saturated. He never said it was not worth publishing, but I was discouraged. I sent it to Nebraska, Oklahoma, Texas, Virginia—virtually every place, it seemed, that had a viable press at the time. There were eight of them, and they all said the same thing: "We cannot sell enough copies." That's when I lost my innocence with some university presses, because I thought that was what they were in business to do was to publish things the market might not sustain. But they all were already into where they definitely are now, and that is they have to be self-sustaining because their host institutions do not give them much but quarters anymore. They are lucky sometimes if they get that. But in any event, no offense to Texas A&M University Press; I think they know what I'm talking about.

In any event, I ran into Bill Wiley, a distinguished Civil War scholar from the 1930s and 1940s, when he received an award in Houston. Judy and I drove down to Houston to see Wiley again and also to visit with Vandiver and others. When he asked about the Hotchkiss diary and I told him the story, he suggested I send it to SMU. He said, "I'm on the board up there and I think they're probably looking for good manuscripts, and I know that's a good one." So I sent it to Dallas, and Allen Maxwell was the director and Margaret Hartley was the editor. I had never been through the rigors of university press editing, but I can say there are not many major professors in the world who can wield a red pen like Margaret Hartley could. But along the way, there was a major bump in the road. I got a note from her saying they had run out of money and could no longer publish it, so she offered to return my manuscript. I wrote her back and said, "Quite honestly, I can't place it anywhere else, so why don't you just keep it and maybe someday you'll get the money?" Three years later I get a letter from Margaret in the early part of the year, and she said they had a late-year tax donation from a wealthy supporter who was a Civil War buff, so they would publish my book instead of some others that were ahead of it in line. I never learned the donor's name. It was sort of like that Walter Prescott Webb and J. H. Hines story, and I wanted to buy into that type of thing, but I was never able to learn his name. Anyway, she said I would have to revise all the footnotes, since so much other work had come out by then, so I got busy. It was finally published in 1973, thanks to a lot of good folks like Vandiver and Williams.

It worked out and is still in print, and the press sells about a thousand copies a year. The fact is that it is about Virginia, and lots and lots of people in Virginia are still fighting the Civil War.

CHAPTER 3

Heading West to East Texas

My last semester at LSU, I was substituting for Dr. John Loos, a distinguished faculty member who was on leave, so I had two full sections of US history and also taught an extension course at Franklin, Louisiana, two nights a week. The reason for all that financial exigency is that Judy had become pregnant with what was our first child, Tucker, who was born the first week of April 1963. It was about that time that I heard about the job opening at Murray State University in western Kentucky. It is just below Paducah and about ten miles north of the Tennessee state line. It was beautiful country where they grew a lot of tobacco. I got the job really through the young woman who was assigned to be the grader in my class that spring—a former Miss Kentucky, I might add—who was in the master's program at LSU and a graduate of Murray. I joined a social science faculty of fifteen, which included sociologists, economists, political scientists, and nine history teachers. I taught five classes: three on a Monday, Wednesday, Friday, and then on Tuesday, Thursday, I taught two and also completed my dissertation that year. With a new baby, too, that was kind of a full year. Murray is a wonderful school, and I probably could have made a career there and would have been quite happy to do so.

There was a bit of a disappointment for me in that they had hired that same year an instructor named Patrick Bledsoe, who was given the Civil War courses I had hoped to teach. He was hired first, though, and I understood that. I got to teach southern and western history, and some US history survey courses, and learned probably more than I taught about those subjects in those days. But in any event, what really brought us back to Texas was of course that we were both Texans and we had this new child, and we were seven hundred miles away from two sets of grandparents. I learned of an opening at Stephen F. Austin State Teachers College through a telephone call, probably in March 1964, from Carl L. Davis. Carl had been a graduate student at Rice when I was there and he was close to the department chairman, Dr. C. K. "Dick" Chamberlain, and in fact he handled a lot of administrative things for Chamberlain in those days. The university was growing so rapidly then that they desperately needed faculty, particularly in the service courses that everybody had to take, such as English, history, and political science. So, Davis called and said, "Would you like a job?" I told him I would love to come back to Texas, and he said, "Well, get down here as fast as you can and talk to Dr. Chamberlain." So we went home to Beaumont on Easter break, and then one day I drove up to Nacogdoches early in the morning and met Dr. Chamberlain. We visited for a while and he made me an offer, which represented a significant raise in salary from what I was making. I was still not going to get to teach Civil War because Jim Nichols taught those classes, so I learned a lot of other subjects at that point. But nonetheless, it was a lot closer to those grandparents and it was in Texas, which was also a goal of ours. We went over to meet Dr. Ralph Steen, and then Dr. Chamberlain took me to the Rotary club. When we got back, they offered me the job. That's how fast all that went, so I returned home to Texas.

The way I was hired was not unusual in those days. It was typical to meet colleagues after they were hired, because Chamberlain or someone else had met them at a conference of the Southern Historical Association (Mississippi Valley Historical Association in those days) or the Organization of American Historians, or some other group, and then hired them and they just showed up on campus one day. The surprising thing is that it all worked out very well. We had a really good department then and still do, although most of those I am speaking of are gone now. In any event, I went back to Murray and gave them the news I was leaving, and they seemed genuinely disappointed, particularly Frank Steely, who was sort of the straw boss of the historians. He, of course, knew he had to find a replacement.

Once we made the decision to move to Nacogdoches, we started traveling to see as much of the area around western Kentucky as we could. On one of those trips we went down to the southern part of Tennessee and the northern part of Mississippi in the Civil War battlefield area. One day, we had just finished visiting Shiloh and were coming up out of the battlefield onto the highway, still wondering how we were going to relocate to East Texas, and at that point a moving van went by emblazoned with the words "Christian Movers, Nacogdoches, Texas." So, we got in touch with them and made the dates in August when we would come to Nacogdoches. They showed up two days early, because the guy who drove the truck was from Nacogdoches and he was anxious to get home since he had been gone all summer. We first lived over at 904 Durst Street here in Nacogdoches in an old house that was peculiar in many ways, like it had seven rooms and no hallway. All the rooms connected to each other. We lived there for two years while we saved the down payment for our house on Redbud Street.

There was just Judy and me and our son, Tucker, then. It was time to get him back to Texas, where he belonged, because he was born in Baton Rouge over Texas soil. As it came time for him to arrive, Judy was obviously going to deliver in Baton Rouge, and we were both such incurable Texans that she determined he would have to be born over Texas soil. So, on a trip home, we got a fruit jar full of dirt from Newton County, which is where Judy's dad and mother had a place, up near Bon Wier. One of the final things she and her mother did before it came time for the delivery was to make up some little bags for some of the dirt along with an announcement for Tucker that he had been born over Texas soil and that she had convinced the obstetrician, who was from Arkansas and who understood state pride, I guess. He actually taped one of those little packages under the table where Tucker was delivered. You may think that is peculiar, but when Judy served as mayor of Nacogdoches, one of the final things she did before she relinquished the office was attend a White House conference in Washington. President Clinton was in office, but there were lots of other people there who were at the conference. One of them was Linda Bird Johnson Robb, Lyndon B. Johnson's daughter and at that time wife of the former senator from Virginia. They got to talking there and it turned out that, as she said, "Daddy made me do the same thing," because their child was born in Maryland, but she said he brought in a whole potted plant. So, LBJ topped me on that one.

When we learned we were going to have a second child—who we named Christopher—we built a house in a subdivision called Austin Heights, which was developed by a man named Trammel Lacey who used to run a cotton gin in Nacogdoches. When the cotton business played out, he became a developer. We built that house and lived there for thirty-seven years before we moved down by the creeks.

We came in the fall of 1964, and my first encounter with the East Texas Historical Association (ETHA) was on October 10 of that year. The ETHA conference was coming up and the program was not yet finalized, so I was told I was going to give a paper. I said, "But I don't know anything about East Texas. I'm a Civil War historian and I've been studying the war in Virginia for the last five years. What can I talk about?" So Jim Nichols told me I could talk about the Texas broiler industry, which developed here after World War II and is still today a fairly prominent business. He offered to teach me about the industry, so he coached me and told me what to say, virtually, and I delivered my paper on that Saturday morning. In those days the association met only on Saturday morning, concluding with a luncheon. The board met in the morning and then the sessions started at nine. There would probably be one or two papers at nine and then two more at 10:45, and then the luncheon.

We met on the university campus, and I suspect there were no more than seventy-five people in attendance. Even though that was still relatively young in the association's life, they started off with about four hundred charter members because they left the membership open for a whole year.

The University Center was in the same location, although it is not the same building because there have been so many renovations that very little of the original building remains. It is a large and sprawling building now but was much smaller in those days. The university did not charge for the use of the room, which was crucial to the meeting, because in those days everything was on a shoestring in terms of the amount of available money. One of the arrangements in those days was that the university paid for the publishing of the *East Texas Historical Journal* and the association provided whatever secretarial or other assistance they could. Most often the History Department's secretary and faculty members donated their time.

By the way, my broiler presentation was my first professional paper for any meeting. As a graduate student I had been invited to Civil War Round Tables by both Frank Vandiver and Harry Williams in Houston and Baton Rouge, and at one of those I was asked to comment on my dissertation, but there was no formal paper. The only writing I had done at that point was a book review for the *Baton Rouge Morning Advocate* of a juvenile Civil War novel. Harry Williams did a weekly review every Sunday in the newspaper there, and occasionally when they would send him a book he preferred not to mess with, he would assign it to a graduate assistant. I still have that book.

In any event, that was the only writing for publication I had ever done before, so delivering my paper at ETHA was a real baptism into professional activity. I was absolutely frightened. I had no idea what I was really talking about. I was repeating things Jim Nichols told me, and had he wanted to embarrass me he could have given me all kinds of fallacious information. But as no one stoned me or anything, I assumed he gave me good material, but I was absolutely frightened and I'm not sure I had much breakfast that morning.

I had attended conferences before, like the one for the Southern Historical Association, but I was job hunting then and just in awe of the great stars of the profession. Bill Wiley was one of the stars in those days. C. Vann Woodward then was a demigod that was off somewhere in North Carolina having written *The Strange Career of Jim Crow*. Folks like William Hesseltine, Harry Williams, Bill Wiley, and E. Merton Coulter would all mill around in the lobby, and their satellites—the younger scholars—would circle around them looking for favors or crumbs. Vandiver was, of course, a part of that inner sanctum, too.

I had only limited experience with regional associations as well. When I was at LSU, Baton Rouge was the headquarters of the Louisiana Historical Association, and the editor of the journal was Edwin A. Davis, who was the History Department chairman. Otis Hebert was his assistant and later became the director. Hebert and I shared an office during the time that I was teaching for John Loos, so I was a little bit familiar with their operation. It was all new to me and I was not sufficiently clued in to the group's significance or to the role it played. I had a big learning curve to overcome with regard to such organizations.

And that takes me back to ETHA, which is where my perspective began to change. I worked for the man who was running it, and prudence dictated that one would do that sort of thing, so I joined. At the time, the association was virtually run out of Dr. Chamberlain's back pocket. He was a true man about town; he was a prominent Rotarian and had headed the Easter Seal

Campaign. He was also active in the Democratic Party. Because he was so busy, though, he would just sort of realize that we had a meeting coming up in a month and that we needed to get everything organized. Then it was all hands on deck until we could get the program together, make all the arrangements, and see that it all floated smoothly, but it was important to him. The longer he was at it, the more important it became to him, which made his departure sort of bitter on his part. There were just so many other things he had to do and it took its place in that order instead of being the primary thing he did most every day. It worked, though, and it was small enough then that no one was displeased by his method. I think this is what they expected.

The primary players, in terms of the professionals who gave papers, came from places like East Texas State, Sam Houston, Lamar, and SFA, but Chamberlain always made sure there was room for the laity. Lay historians have always been crucial to the organization, and I think it is meaningful and helpful to the Texas State Historical Association and to any other major regional or national association, although there are certainly those, like Southwest Social Sciences, where the participants are primarily professionals, but in an organization like ours, the laity is integral. That is why I always made sure that each journal included lay representation. They liked to see their names in print, and their opinions are as valid as anyone else's, and the readers like to see their opinions. The converse is true as well, though, in that readers also want to see an expert's opinion. Just like with lawyers and doctors, there are times you seek out the professional expert, so I included those opinions as well.

It was not long before I became more involved in ETHA. As I mentioned, Jim Nichols was already teaching the Civil War at SFA, so I was given the topics others did not necessarily want. I taught American Colonial history and American Revolutionary history, which I eventually convinced them to combine as one course. I taught two halves of American social and cultural history. I also urged the department to let me teach historiography because that was far and away the most significant course I took in my graduate instruction. That is where I learned how to be a historian. The subject matter you take for granted; you are supposed to learn that, but that historiography course was absolutely critical. I modeled it somewhat on what LSU and Rice did, and that included a lot of philosophy of history, but John Loos took it further and taught a course heavy on bibliography, learning where things were in the library and how to use them, and also how to research the biographies of historians to learn how they lived and what perspectives they represented. I have long taught some of the things I learned about Charles Austin Beard and the economic interpretation of history, about Frederick Jackson Turner and the frontier thesis, and about Walter Webb and the Great Plains and the metropolis concept. I learned about those ideas through my historiography class. I thought our graduate students needed to know about bibliographies and how to use and appreciate libraries. The only way you can really learn that or master it is to physically go to a library and find out about the books located there. I would tell my students to handle the books, to look inside to see who wrote them, who published them, when they were published, and what the contents were—those are the things I wanted them to learn. I have had a lot of students decry the bibliographic study, and one who is a dear friend now still refers to it as "that damn bibliography."

I continued to teach all of those courses and was still doing that when Dr. Chamberlain reached the age of seventy. That was before the Supreme Court ruled there is no such thing as compulsory retirement, with obviously the exceptions of firemen, airline pilots, and a few people like that, but certainly not sedentary college professors. So, Chamberlain had no choice but to comply with the rule and retire, whether it was a state or university rule. He was still healthy and vigorous, and there was no real reason why he had to retire, except to follow the rule. He moved his books out of his office, and eventually Robert Maxwell moved in, but Chamberlain just left them in boxes in the hall and it was a long, long time before they were removed. He assumed he would go on being director of the association and that giving up the chairmanship of the History Department was unrelated. I guess to his great disappointment he discovered they were together, at least in the way the university administration viewed the matter. His last meeting was in September 1971, and sadly, he was killed in an automobile accident about a year after he ceased to be editor, which was then the title for the position now known as director. At the time Chamberlain left, James Nichols was the ETHA president and Lee Lawrence was still a member of the board, and it was with those two that I interviewed. They asked Bobby Johnson and me to come over on a Saturday to an ETHA board meeting, and they interviewed us both.

Bobby H. Johnson—he is not a Robert—was an esteemed colleague of mine at SFA. He came to the university in the mid-1960s and was a western historian. He attended the University of Oklahoma, and he had been a reporter for the Abilene newspaper and edited the Abilene Christian College newspaper, and he had worked at Harding College in Arkansas in a journalistic capacity. He was very familiar with the publication process, more so than I. My journalistic experience was limited to editing the newspaper at French High School. For whatever reasons, though, they selected me, and importantly, Bobby and I remained friends. He was very gracious about the whole thing.

I really believe the decision was made by Lee Lawrence and Ralph Steen. I suspect those two just decided to lay the sword down on my shoulder and that was all there was to it, even though there was a vote by the board. I was greatly honored in the first place to be considered and thought I was competent enough to take on the assignment. It brought a lot of statewide attention to both me and the university and it gave me a new forum. I sat in judgment in a way on what articles we published, what books we reviewed and who reviewed them, and then who got to present papers at the meetings. Many times, even though we worked through program chairs, I would be asked to recruit some of the speakers. It gave me some responsibility within our niche of Texana, and that I think is what enabled me to move on into the broader aspect of Texas history. Again, Lee Lawrence was my patron in that regard.

One important benefit that attracted me to the job was that it brought a reduction in my regular teaching load, which consisted of four courses a semester. Such reductions were not as common then as they are now, and mine extended on into the summer, which was crucial. Summer enrollment levels were higher then, because we had a lot of teachers who took advantage of the break to work on graduate degrees, but that declined through the years because of differences in scheduling. Regardless, I needed the extra time, because the summer break was the busiest time for the editor and director. If the director is arranging the fall meeting as well as getting ready the following spring journal, he or she is as busy or busier during the month of August than any other month of the year, so that was important to me. I later was able to get that reduced to a six-hour load because of the great increase in the volume of duties, and that was where I was when I retired from the position.

When I started as director, I visited with President Steen about how we were going to manage everything, and at that point he gave me the news that the university would no longer pay for printing the journal. As he said, "The association is way down the totem pole here with the state printer. You're part of SFA's business, but any other state agency has priority over you." One of the reasons why the journal was coming out six months behind is that the printer was just doing it on a timely basis. But, Steen added, "If you pay the bill, you select the printer, and you're the customer; you're in a position to really give them deadlines to meet if they want to keep the business." And, he added, "I'll pay the secretary," which in those days was a half-time student, "and you pay your own printing bill." We had around $1,500, which was about what it would cost to print one issue of the journal. At that point we did not have enough money to even print the second issue of that volume because it comes out biannually. Somehow, though, we raised the necessary funds through dues, meeting revenues, and other means, and we were even able to get a bit ahead, and that continued for some time. Before we were able to develop endowments, though, we were just paying the bills.

One early change I instituted to help us out was to replace the October and March dates on the journal spine with Spring and Fall—much bigger targets. I also revised the internal schedule so we could mail out the journal along with the meeting program and registration in order to save postage. To facilitate that, we moved the meetings to September and February. Now, February is not really spring yet and is a little closer to September than September is to the following February, but it fit the academic calendar better and it got us out of conflict with the Texas State Historical Association's meeting, which was always the first week of March. The only other early conflict we had was with the state association of junior colleges, and they often met on the same weekend we did and we probably had a heavier concentration of junior college membership then than we do now, so they asked us to move our date, and we did, because we had more flexibility. After making that change, though, I could not believe that the next year they moved theirs up a week, so after that I just decided we had to punt to keep from moving around every year. Our members had to have a target date in order to plan their schedules, so we set it up for the third weekend of September or the third weekend in February to be as consistent as we could. There were at times conflicts we could not resolve, primarily with the hotel bookings, but most people benefited from having a fairly predictable schedule, and we have adhered to that for more than thirty-five years.

With regard to the journal, I viewed it primarily as a deadline matter. I had to acquire a certain number of articles and get them to the publisher by a specific date. To a large degree I was dependent on the articles I received, but I also had to be open to the breadth of possible history in the region. A case in point is that a few years ago Bruce Glasrud called my attention to the fact that the East Texas Historical Association in my tenure had published forty-one articles on African American history and far exceeded the number of articles on that subject published by any other historical publication in the nation except the *Journal of Negro History*. That was on my part absolutely unconscious; I did not set out to meet that objective, but it came from our people who write, and I respected their contributions. At the same time, I had to monitor the frequency of topical stories. I wanted to avoid duplicate efforts and repetition, but at times I would also group stories together in a special issue. At one point, for example, I did a whole issue on African American history, and one on women's history, and another on forestry. In general, though, I published what was sent to me that was good enough to publish and would fit our format. We have a ninety-six-page format, so I can budget about five articles if they average in manuscript length about twenty pages each. That leaves me enough pages for book reviews, a news column, and the end matter that is required. In the process, I was reflecting what the profession was doing and going through in those times.

In the early days of my directorship, the quality of the available articles was not bad, but it was uneven. In general, we received good articles from the history professionals, and through the years we have had some remarkably gifted writers in the laity. We have additionally had some historians who knew their subject pretty well but failed to achieve the "felicity of languages," as university press editor Frank Wardlaw used to say. When I took over, I only had four or five submissions to work with, and a couple of those were really not acceptable. With what I inherited, if I was unsure how I could use it, I just acted like it never existed, because that was an easy way out. I felt I was under no obligation to respond because they had not been submitted to me and I wanted to avoid hurting the authors' feelings, so I just did nothing about them. Those I had that were good and deemed publishable, I published. I solicited some as well if I knew someone who was working on a specific topic or had competence in certain areas, and many of those people had no prior intention of writing but were just interested, and some of them produced good articles.

I had to be a recruiter for articles as well as book reviews. I was particularly proud of how the book review section developed. I remember one time Dr. Dorman Winfrey, a respected historian from Henderson and for many years the state archivist, wrote me a complimentary letter to express his opinion that we had the best book review section of any journal in Texas. I think one thing he noticed was that I never disallowed a book on Texas just because it was not specifically about East Texas. Almost any book on the state, after all, is going to have some connection to East Texas. More importantly, our members were interested in all of Texas history, not just in their region. We were a geographic convenience, we were a source of local pride and interest, and so forth, but our people are Texas historians and so are going to be interested in something whether or not it is specifically about East Texas.

I did hope there would be some kind of connection, and I did that with articles as well, but in terms of the book reviews, I went to Houston and spent a day with Sanford "Hig" Higginbotham, who was the editor of the *Journal of Southern History* at Rice. The *Journal of Southern History* had been brought to Rice while I was a graduate student and it was my first experience with journal production. When the books would come in for review, graduate students would literally riff through every copy to make sure the pages were all printed. I guess in the past they had experienced some problems in that regard. Then we would stuff them into envelopes and put them into big gray mailbags and drag them to the post office. That was the extent of my experience with journals, so I needed to work with Hig on what I should do. He was very gracious and walked me through the whole thing, and I used his procedures to set up our own. I came home with a copy of his instructions to book reviewers, for example, and with his permission I just changed the *Journal of Southern History* to *East Texas Historical Journal*. If there is an editor's school, that's where I went that one day with Hig. I took away a wealth of information, some of which I applied directly, some of which evolved with my own style over time. There were others who influenced my style, notably Ouida Whitaker Dean and Peter von Wahlide, who I will discuss in more detail later.

In setting up the journals, I learned to date articles as I accepted them and to publish them in that order, although there were a few important exceptions. For example, if Max Lale sent me something, it appeared in the next journal as the lead article, because that was politics. Max was such a wonderful man, and he was the heart and soul of the historical community of Harrison County until the day he died, even though the last five years of his life he resided in Fort Worth. He was extremely generous to the association not only with his money, which was crucial in establishing the Lale Lecture Series, but also with his influence, understanding, and support of me. So, while some might be critical of that preferential treatment, it was how I chose to operate to benefit the association in the long run. Max was generous, too, in terms of sharing people that he knew, and he knew some important people.

Another member who was also influential in that regard for the longest time was Bob Bowman. For similar reasons he was very supportive of me, and he was very generous with the association, particularly through grants from the Pineywoods Foundation for symposia and other projects. He designed the cover of the *East Texas Historical Journal* that we used the last twenty-five years I was the editor.

Also important in the early days was Lucille Terry of Jefferson. She had inherited the preservation mantle of Ruth Lester up there and spearheaded the Excelsior Hotel operation. Another strong supporter of the association was Maury Darst, who was from Nacogdoches and a graduate of SFA, but he taught at Galveston College. There was also Irvin May, who started out at Texas A&M and then went to Blinn College. He was also an East Texan, and I think until the day he died he still owned the family property near Overton. He would come over every now and then to get a "pine tree fix," as I called it. He actually gave us our very first bequest in a will, and he was always supportive of our efforts. The Beaumont contingent of supporters, as I might label them, was headed by Ralph Wooster of Lamar University, but also important was Preston Williams. We have always had a strong Beaumont contingent.

Governor Price Daniel of Liberty was supportive of me personally, though not necessarily through the association. I cherish a picture of the two of us standing in front of the Robertson house in Salado. He was the presiding officer at the annual book event there in the Stagecoach Inn, and I was one of the speakers. In the photo I was wearing this god-awful polyester suit, and I had a shock of hair that made me look like Conway Twitty, with sideburns down to my lower jaw—quite a contrast to Daniel standing there in his elegance, but we became friends. I originally met him through service on Mary Pearson's board for the Texas county records inventory project, and Daniel was a strong supporter of that effort. He was a governor who understood history and was married to a descendant of Sam Houston as well. When I heard him make a talk one time, he said he had taken an oath of office or loyalty to the Texas and the US Constitution eleven times through all the various offices he held. He was a grand man who loved Texas history, and he is the reason we have a State Archives building in Austin right there beside the Capitol. That was his pet project.

And while I am thinking about people who were influential in the early days of the association, I need to recognize Tommie Jan Lowery, who was the association secretary and who personally provided generous funding for a lot of our work. That informal arrangement came into question to some degree at my first board meeting. Dr. Robert Cotner was the association president at the time. He was a professor at the University of Texas, the distinguished biographer of Governor James Stephen Hogg, and a prominent Texas historian. Since our finances were no longer going to be processed through the History Department, we had to pay more of our bills, so Tommie and I thought we needed a petty cash fund for office supplies. The idea of having cash in the office, however, was not something Cotner cottoned to. He was not accusing us or even suspecting us of theft, but it was just an alien concept to him. As I recall, it bothered Tommie, who was wealthy and therefore offended that she could even be tempted by a petty cash fund, but he refused, so it became a real issue of how we were going to operate. It was a rocky time, and perhaps it was in part a reflection of the fact I was an unproven commodity, but we eventually got past that roadblock. What I learned in the process was that I had to be careful not to just go on and do things unilaterally but to remember that the board should be providing approval. Toward the end of my career, though, I knew what had to be done and knew to act judiciously when we had no alternative choice, so I would sometimes take on more of that responsibility. Overall, though, the board and I had to trust each other.

The matter of trust was particularly important when Tommie Jan Lowery later decided to quit. She had been there from the beginning, but when we started having to be accountable for all funds, she no longer felt comfortable handling expenses out of her own purse, so she wanted out as the association treasurer. The only thing of convenience and practicality was for the board to name my secretary to that position, because one thing I determined from the beginning was that I would not handle money. If someone paid me their dues in person, for example, I made sure someone saw me turn the money over to the treasurer or my secretary. I did have to make the decisions on how we would spend money, but someone else had to sign the checks. I wanted to be sure we had that system of balance and transparency.

The secretary position went from part time to full time as I took on more responsibilities. Many of the first ones I worked with were students, whose priorities were understandably their studies. When I also became editor of a publication called *Encyclopedia U.S.A.*, I went to the college president, William R. Johnson, and asked for more secretarial assistance, which he granted. Later when I gave up the encyclopedia work because the ETHA work had expanded, I again returned to visit with Johnson. I remember he got out the budget and was looking through it, and he said, "What are you really asking for?" I said I just wanted to keep things like they were, and he just folded it up and put it down and said, "Oh, I thought you were asking for something to do and I couldn't do that, but if we're going to keep things like we are, then everything is all right."

One early secretary who should be mentioned is Karen Gehring, who worked with the association for seven years. Now, we sometimes had to talk about who was director and who was not, but she was a very supportive person and extremely religious. I have no objection to any religion, by the way, and I practice some of it myself, but she supported Pat Robertson for president, so we never discussed religion or politics, but she was a great secretary. I had to dismiss one secretary who lied to me, but I will not dwell on that. The good news is that I was rewarded soon after by the best secretary I ever had, and that is Mrs. Portia Gordon. We have now been together fifteen years—thirteen with the association and two with my work as university liaison.

CHAPTER 4

The Editor's Cut

When I began working for ETHA, the only title was editor, but there was really no formal editorial philosophy, so I had to develop my own. Generally, I just followed common sense, but I also borrowed from the work of Ouida Whitaker Dean, a gifted editor who helped me with my biography of William Barret Travis. An active member of the association, she was an English teacher at Timpson High School at the time and one of the great masters of the grammar of the English language. In fact, when we finished with the Travis manuscript, I framed one of her edited pages. I failed to actually count her corrections, but I literally believe she wrote more on that page than I did, correcting my syntax, sentence structure, and subject-verb agreement, with better adjectives than I had, and so forth. So I learned a great deal about just techniques from her and probably equally from a man named Peter von Wahlide. Peter was a Russian historian who joyfully told me the first time I met him, when I was prospecting to go to work for him as editor of *Encyclopedia U.S.A.*, that he had been fired from every teaching job he ever had. His solution to that was to form his own company, and he published *Encyclopedia U.S.A.* I edited the first volume and sent it to him, and within three or four days it came back to me as unacceptable. So I went to Pensacola, near his home in Gulf Breeze across the bay, and worked with him three or four days. We went over that by page by page and line by line, and I probably learned ultimately more about copyediting directly from Peter than I did from any other one source. Now sometimes I had to get in his face, because he did not give criticism graciously. He was fairly direct in his opinions about my work, and he let me know in no uncertain terms. I could take that up to a degree, but there would come a point where my temper would come into play and I had to tell him, "If you do that one more time, we're not only through, but we're probably going to fight right here." And he would always look so wounded, but he grew to understand he had hurt my feelings. He would apologize and we would continue for a while and then go back at it, and it would happen all over again. But anyway, he was the best. I have always said he is the best copyeditor I have seen anywhere.

You know, I hope a lot of that rubbed off on me. One of the great compliments came from a friend of mine who once asked, "Why do all the articles read alike, as if they are written by the same person?" And I said, "Well, I guess I rewrite them all." I wasn't consciously damaging anybody's style; I was just trying to improve each one so the verbs agreed and the adjectives were correct and in the right place, and the language was precise with punctuation that would be consistent.

Particularly in the early days we had some editorial pushback from some folks who had been prominent in the formation of the association and who had a proprietary attitude about their work. They sort of automatically expected what they sent in to be printed without changes. I must admit I did some of that. Sometimes it was good politics for the association and maybe even selfish for me at that point. I think in an association like ours where the lay membership is at least equal numerically, and more equal in their tangible support of the organization, that they do have a right to be represented. So I purposefully made sure that every issue would have an article by a lay historian. I also made sure that I had plenty of representation from lay book reviewers. They liked to see their names in print, and their opinions are as valid as anyone's, and furthermore, people like them like to see their opinions. They also want to see the opinions of the professional historian, but I tried to make sure that both of those avenues were satisfied.

Coincidentally, the most controversial thing I ever had to deal with as editor involved a book review. The book was on more of a South Texas topic than an East Texas topic, but part of my philosophy was that while we may have been the East Texas Historical Association, I assumed that, like myself, the majority of our membership was interested in all of Texas history, so if you live in Jasper you can still be concerned with what's going on in Austin. This is something else I got from Hig Higginbotham, by the way.

Hig did an article in the *Journal of Southern History* on populism in Kansas. In it he noted Kansas is not the South, but that populism is very important in the South. This was about the origins of it, so he figured people in Atlanta would like to read it, too. So, in a similar way, we always had plenty of other Texas regions in the journal.

Anyway, the lady who reviewed this particular South Texas book [the two-volume *History of Refugio* by Hobart Huson] had been a colleague of mine in graduate school at Rice and was from Corpus Christi. In her review she was critical of the book. Normally the policy is that if there is a particularly critical book review and there is a protest from the author of the book, you offer the author an opportunity to respond and then you offer the reviewer an attempt to respond to the response or rebuttal and you publish them simultaneously, side by side, or at least consecutively in the next journal. The protest came not from Mr. Huson—I never heard from him—but rather from a federal judge in the district involving San Antonio, Austin, and El Paso. The judge called me on the telephone and read me the riot act. A friend of the author, he had some very unkind things to say about the judgment of the reviewer, and he wanted an immediate retraction. I explained what the normal procedure was, but I also said to him, "I'm not really sure how to proceed here because you are neither the author nor the reviewer. You are an interested third party." And by the way, he kept bantering about this word *libel*, and finally I got maybe as pushy as I got with a federal judge, and I said, "Now judge, you and I both know the definition of libel, and this ain't it. This is not libelous; this is an opinion of a work and that's not what libel is." And he granted me that, but I did say to him, "Because you feel so passionately about this, I will let you take the place of the author and write the rebuttal, but I must let the reviewer respond to that, and they'll be published simultaneously." This went on through several telephone conversations and communications, and by the way it's a little unnerving when somebody on the other end of the line asks if you will hold for a federal judge. Eventually, though, he finally said well enough and sent a handwritten, multipage response to the review. In his note, he said he would be happy if I would just share it with the reviewer. He did not want it published, but he said she should see the response so "she will know she is wrong." I agreed to do that and I let her know I would be forwarding it to her. She was not happy and instead was ready to fight, but I responded, "Please just accept this. You don't have to respond and you don't even have to open the letter. I'm going to send it and let's just let it go away." The end of the story is that this is the judge who was shot in San Antonio, and so I often wondered what the FBI was going to say when they found the correspondence while looking for all of his enemies. I hope, though, that I was always gentlemanly and professional in my response.

That was the single most controversial thing I had to deal with, but I often received submissions for articles that did not meet our standards. One, for example, was just a list of everybody who had served in a particular Confederate unit in the Civil War. While that has some merit genealogically, and a lot of our members have interests in family history, the journal was not a genealogical publication. We had to have some context and some relevance that would make it interesting for everybody else, but this one happened to come from a particularly significant founder of the association. So I just put it in the file and said I would publish it when I got the time and the space, and it just never happened, you know. It just never happened. I always tried to treat people with kindness, and I always tried to spare their feelings if I could.

As I mentioned in terms of editorial philosophy, I always tried to make sure the laity were represented. The other side of that is that I also wanted the works to be of as good a quality as they could be. I liked annotation, because it showed the tracks of the research, but I also did not check every source. Historian Wendell Holmes Stephenson, editor of the *Journal of Southern History* and the *Mississippi Valley Historical Review*, was also editor of a ten-volume series entitled *The History of the South*. I was in a meeting with him one time, and our friend Haskell Monroe asked him which volume he thought was the best. Unquestionably, he observed, it was the one by C. Vann Woodward, because he only made four errors in his footnotes. Stephenson had literally checked every footnote to find the documentation errors. Noting that Woodward was as familiar with the literature of the South as anybody, he might note a wrong publication date, relying solely on his memory. I had too many classes to teach to be able to do that and I was too far from the library but I liked to see the footnotes, even though I would at times accept articles that were simply undocumented essays. I appreciated those who used footnotes, though, because it at least showed someone was willing to be checked had I had the opportunity to do that. Regardless, I am sure there were errors that crept in through the years.

In reviewing an article, what was immediately important to me was the topic. Was it pertinent to the publication? It might meet other criteria, but if it did not conform to the purpose of the journal, it really should not be published. Also relevant at times, though, was the author. There are some people who, by their preeminence in a particular field of history, would make significant contributions to the prestige of the publication. Conversely, there are some people who no one might recognize as a historian, but who are nonetheless important to the organization. I had a member one time who sent me lots of things that were not accepted for other publications but which I thought were quite good enough to publish in the journal. I would publish his material even though it did not necessarily meet editorial criteria, because he was vitally important to the association. He was important in a collegial sense but also in a financial sense, so the old adage held—"If it bleeds, it leads." If this man sent me something, it led the next issue because of my great respect for him.

I would, at times, produce special themed issues, based largely on the preponderance of topics I received at the time. There was one on women's history, one on African American history, and still another on Reconstruction. I could have strung them out over several years in several editions, but I chose to do several at once and then not go back to that general topic until a reasonable time had expired and other topics had been given a chance to be considered. Sometimes that led into a distinction that I never intended. I was floored when historian Bruce Glasrud did a survey of journals we had put out over a period of thirty-something years and learned that we had published forty-one articles on African American history. I would like to know if there were similar effects on other topics, such as women's history or sawmill history. The results might be equally impressive.

In the early days of the journal, when I would work through concerns over topics and personalities, a lot had to do with the physical condition or format of the piece. Before the widespread use of computers and printers, I often got handwritten submittals and some typed on different sizes of paper. If it was typed legibly it was just easier to work with, and that was an advantage to the author. With handwritten book reviews or those that were not carefully typed I was afraid I might publish something that was not intended. Then there were the occasional articles that at first glance appeared way too long for the journal. I occasionally made exceptions, and one of those was for an extensive annotated bibliography compiled by Daniel J. Gelo and Tammy J. Morales on the Alabama and Coushatta tribes of East Texas. I liked to have four or five articles per issue, plus twenty to thirty reviews, and I had a budget of about ninety-six pages to work with, including the cover and other front and back matter. That one article would have taken up half the issue and cut down considerably on what else I could include, but I ended up publishing it because I felt it was the only place that bibliography was ever going to be published, so I wanted the journal to be the source. We published it as one article and not as a series. Of course, bibliographies are dated the minute you publish them because somebody is always working on new sources, but at least for that time it was a snapshot of everything that was available on that particular day.

Book reviews were often difficult to plan for, because they varied so in length. The mental gymnastics of trying to keep all that in order was often trying. The solution, though, was that I always sent three reviews more than I thought we were going to need. The understanding with the printer was that if he needed them, he could use them, or he could leave them out depending on his space needs. To help him out, I would list them in the way I really thought they ought to be done. When laying out the reviews, I tried to follow a certain chronology. If they were really general works, they led, followed by the Spanish, Mexican, and Anglo periods of East Texas and then the nineteenth- and twentieth-century books. Then at the end I would include books that were difficult to categorize chronologically, like one on the pine tree or something of that nature. Then I would have the adjustable part where it would cause no harm if the reviews were left out.

When analyzing the proposed articles and determining which were right for the journal, I addressed each piece individually. I liked to have good narrative; I liked to have a beginning and an ending. I was a historicist I guess in that I judged everything on its own merits based on what it purported to do. Obviously, part of that ultimate judgment was how well it was done, and how well it was done would have to do with writing with conception—and length again, because you can take an infinitesimal little thing and write thirty pages about it or you can take something like the

Civil War and sum it up in a paragraph. There are extremes, but how did the author balance the stuff in between? My personal preference was to find out other people's personal preferences. That is, I liked to know what they were thinking about the subject.

Given all that, there were certain authors I particularly enjoyed working with. Ralph Wooster would be an established name in Texas letters, and I was always glad to receive the things he wrote. I was frequently out to get people such as Frank Vandiver to write for us. Although he never did an article for us, he would do an occasional book review. I was certainly aware of the fact that adding such names brought prestige to our journal, but bigness in the profession nationally or even statewide was not the same thing as bigness where our kind of journal was concerned. I felt our readers liked to see things Lee Lawrence wrote. Lee did not write much, but when he did, like his Camp Ford piece with Bob Glover, they were solid classic studies. His short piece *Texas War Horses*, which he published privately in 1995, would have been good for the journal, but it was, after all, a presidential address for the Texas State Historical Association, so I understood that. Lee was a person who a lot of people knew and respected, so that added prestige to us.

When thinking of some of the more important articles we published, several come to mind. One from Dr. Chamberlain's editorship was Allan C. Ashcraft's definition of East Texas, which has stood the test of time. Allan was a faculty member at Texas A&M University and a prominent member and past president of our association. The most often quoted piece we published was Max Lale's "My War, 1944–1945 (vol. 32, no. 2, 1994). Through the years we received countless inquiries for permission to reprint. Excerpts from that work are included in myriad museum exhibits, including the World War II Museum in New Orleans. Historian Stephen Ambrose was responsible for having it used there and quoted passages extensively, by the way, in *Citizen Soldier*, his book about D-day.

In the early days of the journal we used some unique cover art thanks to Lee Lawrence, who came up with the idea. Lee was of course well connected in the historical community of Texas, and it was he who persuaded the noted artist José Cisneros to draw the map of East Texas that incorporated various historical icons of the region. There was a tree, for example, a missionary ringing a bell, a southern lady, an Indian tepee, a railroad engine, a wagon train, and a longhorn and a mustang, among other images. Interestingly, there was also the image of a lynching along the Trinity River. Lee took care of whatever financial arrangements there were with Cisneros and years later gave me the original signed artwork, which is now with the Stephen F. Austin State University East Texas Research Center. The first cover with the Cisneros artwork came out in 1963.

We had a distinctive yellow cover stock, which was not the result of a design decision but rather a matter of what the printer had in stock at the time. The depth of the color changed somewhat through the years, again based on stock availability.

When I became editor, Dr. Steen called me over and gave me some marching orders. One of the things he pointed out was that the *East Texas Historical Journal* was coming out about six months late, which was a problem since the spines were marked with the months of March and October. Because of the delays at the time, members might get the March issue in October and the October issue the following year, so it was a concern. I solved the problem by broadening the spine dates to Fall and Spring, so that gave us a framework of three months. I never missed a deadline after that.

The other thing Dr. Steen wanted to discuss with me was the matter of printing costs. The association was paying for a secretary and Dr. Steen was paying for the printing costs, as it was technically a bulletin of the university. He offered to pay for the secretary if we would pay for the printing, which was about the same amount of money at the time. He felt that would put us in a position to have more control over service, since we would not be subject to state printing contract restrictions. The contract was then with Craftsman Printers out of Lubbock. I went ahead and took bids from other vendors, but Craftsman still had the best price, and as a result, what developed was one of the most interesting professional relationships I ever experienced. Ronald Peters was the man who ran the company at the time and he pledged to provide the same quality service whether we worked through a state or private agreement. In those days before online publishing, we relied on the mail service completely. We would send him our manuscripts, and he would set the type and send a copy back, which we would proof and return. Then he would send it back in blue line markup, which we checked, and we might do that again before we gave our final approval. This was done in quadrants—eight sections for one journal

—so it took a great deal of time, but once he had our sign-off, he was ready to print. I would give Ronald the date I wanted it delivered and he never missed a deadline. We rocked on through the years, handling most questions via the phone, either with Ronald or his very trusted longtime employee, who I knew only as Lupe. When I called and asked for Ronald, there was never any question about who I was, who I represented, or what I wanted; Ronald would be on the line as quickly as possible. If he was occasionally gone—and he did like to go fishing in Montana once a year—Lupe would be there. We got to where we would talk back and forth to Lupe sometimes just because she was the one who actually made the journal. In the course of those phone conversations, Ronald and I became very close. We would share our joys and concerns and express sympathy for family losses or congratulations for achievements as those things came up in conversation. The point is, I never laid eyes on him or either one of them until near the very end of my tenure when I attended a meeting of the West Texas Historical Association in Lubbock. I called ahead and said, "Ronald if we get there a day early, can we come out and see you?" And he said, "I'll pick you up at the airport." So my colleague Dr. Mark Barringer and I flew out there, and Ronald picked us up and gave us a tour of the plant, which is huge. He prints the city magazine for Los Angeles, as well as other publications out west. He has an impressive and much-in-demand operation, but for whatever reason—I couldn't explain it—he just took an interest in us. The last five years I was editor, he never raised his price once. We made some adjustments after we had computers and the equipment to deliver the journal to him camera-ready, but overall, the price was never different, and in a time when costs were going up 10 and 20 percent on other projects, that was a marvelous assistance to us.

The first major change in the design of the *East Texas Historical Journal* came about in the fall of 1984, primarily through the direction of Bob Bowman, a Lufkin public relations man and an avocational historian. Bob was gaining influence in the association at the time, and it was his opinion that the cover was old-fashioned and that it needed a stronger East Texas image. Given his stature in the organization and the fact I did not at that time have the complete story on the Cisneros artwork, I said, "Let's go ahead. Let's do it." So Bob designed the pine tree cover and I thought it was good. It had the three pine trees on it and it had a consistent color palette, and I think maybe I recommended the blue on gray. One thing that I did was to make the various volumes distinctive. If you put them all on a shelf, they all looked alike and you knew instantly what it was, whereas up to that time the stock color had been all over the map. On the back of the pine tree cover we had our logo, which was a drawing of Dr. Robert W. Glover's cabin, Shiloh, near Flint in Smith County. Bob Glover was a charter member of ETHA, and his cabin was what we would call a double-pen with a dogtrot, or breezeway, in between. The Terry Award we give in recognition of historic preservation bears a likeness of the same cabin.

In the context of the ETHA publications, this is a good place to talk about what became known as the Lawrence Series that was in addition to our journal. Lee Lawrence was a longtime executive council member of TSHA and later president. He had the idea of a small series of monographs, because he said he had spent many a lonely night in a hotel room somewhere in East Texas working on a case, and often out of that grew his interest in knowing more about the history of a place. There were often a few local resources, but those that existed were either oversized or otherwise inadequate for his late-night hotel room research purposes. So, he proposed a series of small monographs that would tell a particular story about a locale. He first proposed the idea to TSHA, which adopted it, and I wrote the first one, entitled *The Old Stone Fort*, about the iconic Nacogdoches structure. Lee left the council with the idea, which had no official name at the time, and the project eventually morphed into the Fred Cotton Series. Cotton was a prominent financial supporter of TSHA, and the directors and editor there decided to name it in his honor. Lee in turn pitched a regional version of the idea to ETHA in the 1990s and we ran with it. He and his wife gave us a certain sum of money to get started, so it became the Ann and Lee Lawrence East Texas History Series. The first publication was *Jefferson: East Texas Metropolis* by Fred Tarpley. Fred was in the English Department at East Texas State University (now Texas A&M University–Commerce). He had a longtime interest in a wide range of topics, including place names, word origins, customs, and so forth, but he had a particular interest in the specific location of the river port town of Jefferson. The second book in the series was *Camp Ford: Tyler, Texas C.S.A.*, by Glover. There were others through the years, like *The Texas and Pacific Depot in Marshall*, by Gail K. Beil and Tom Watson McKinney, and *Steam in the Pines: A History of the Texas State Railroad*, by Jonathan K. Gerland of Lufkin. Then there were two works on the San Augustine area by John and Betty Oglesbee of that town. One was entitled *San Augustine: A Texas Treasure*, and the other was *Reminiscing the Road: El Camino de los Tejas National Historic Trail from Los Adaes to the Trinity River*, which was essentially a historical travelogue of sites along that important Spanish route. The Oglesbees are dear people—true treasures of East Texas. Needless to say, the Lawrences were pleased with the outcome of the series and continued the funding.

While the Lawrence Series was designed to be focused and site-specific, we soon started another publication project for broader works on distinct regional topics. The idea and funding came from Bob and Doris Bowman and was known as the Best of East Texas Series. The first title, published in 2006, was by Bill O'Neal of Carthage and entitled *War in East Texas: Regulators vs. Moderators*. I recruited Bill for that project and he did an excellent job in a relatively short amount of time. The following year we published *The Devil's Triangle: Ben Bickerstaff, Northeast Texans, and the War of Reconstruction* by James Smallwood, Kenneth Howell, and Carol Taylor.

Given the number of publications we produced and the limited size of our staff—myself and an assistant—we made the conscious decision to limit the journal to two issues a year. While we often wanted to do more, we chose to remain focused on quality and not quantity. The journal remained relatively small, as a result, but that fit both the available financial resources and the number of proposed articles we received. The interest by contributing authors remained high through the years and it was rare when I had to go out and beg for a story.

School photo of Archie McDonald. Even at an early age, McDonald wore hats, which would be a part of his personal style throughout his life and also a symbol of his presence at meetings of the East Texas Historical Association (ETHA). *Courtesy Judy McDonald*

A young McDonald on the streets of Beaumont in the 1940s. *Courtesy Judy McDonald*

Archie McDonald at the time of his high school graduation from French High School, Beaumont, 1954. *Courtesy Judy McDonald*

Judy and Archie McDonald at Bay Lake, southeast of Nacogdoches near the old sawmill community of Laceyville, 1971, on the occasion of an Easter sunrise service conducted by Austin Heights Baptist Church. *Courtesy Judy McDonald*

McDonald holding a copy of *Make Me a Map of the Valley: The Civil War Journal of Stonewall Jackson's Topographer* (Southern Methodist University Press, 1973), which he edited. *Courtesy Judy McDonald*

Archie McDonald in his home study, 1968. *Courtesy Judy McDonald*

Judy Barrett McDonald, 1977. Taken by family friend Ouida Whitaker Dean, the picture was part of publicity surrounding Judy's ten years of political service through five elections to the Nacogdoches City Council. *Courtesy Judy McDonald*

F. Lee Lawrence, Tyler attorney, civic leader, historian, and preservationist. Lawrence was instrumental in the early successes of ETHA and served as president, 1962–1963. Like McDonald, he also served as president of the Texas State Historical Association and as a commissioner of the Texas Historical Commission. *Courtesy East Texas Historical Association*

Journalist, author, historian, publicist, and philanthropist Max S. Lale of Marshall and Fort Worth played a key role in keeping ETHA a viable organization through his leadership and financial support. McDonald considered Lale one of his closest friends and advisers. The annual Lale Lecture Series honors the organizational service of Max and his first wife, Georgiana. *Courtesy East Texas Historical Association*

Educator and historian Ralph W. Steen, who grew up in Callahan County in West Texas, provided significant institutional support for ETHA through his position as president of Stephen F. Austin State University from 1958 to 1976. Following retirement, he served as ETHA president, 1978–1979. The organization's award for distinguished service honors his name. *Courtesy East Texas Historical Association*

Judy and Archie in their home kitchen, 2001. SFA photographer Hardy Meredith took this photo as part of the publicity for a reprint of Archie's cookbook, *Helpful Cooking Hints for HouseHusbands of Uppity Women* (E-Heart Press, 1988; reprint, University of North Texas Press, 2001). Written after Judy's election as mayor of Nacogdoches, the book garnered national attention and press coverage for the author. *Courtesy Hardy Meredith, Stephen F. Austin State University*

A family portrait taken aboard a cruise ship on a family vacation to Alaska, circa 2000. Back row, left to right: Chris, Archie, and Tucker McDonald; front row: Judy and Janet McDonald, Tucker's wife; and in the center, appropriately, is Kelly Marie McDonald, daughter of Tucker and Janet. *Courtesy Judy McDonald*

Archie with granddaughter Kelly on a trip to London, 2000. One of Archie's passions was travel, especially heritage tourism, and he greatly enjoyed the times he could share his trips with family. *Courtesy Judy McDonald*

McDonald entertaining guests during a historical marker dedication ceremony commemorating the site of a Civilian Conservation Corps camp at Lufkin, Texas, Valentine's Day, 2007. In reaction to news of the assassination of President John F. Kennedy in 1963, McDonald purchased a four-string guitar and began playing music to soothe his frustration and give voice to his concerns for the nation. Over the years, he developed a program of popular and patriotic World War II–era music that he frequently performed at state and local functions. *Photo by William A. McWhorter, courtesy Texas Historical Commission Military Sites Program, "Texas in World War II" files*

Archie McDonald with former US senator Kay Bailey Hutchison, Nacogdoches, 2007. A lifelong Democrat, McDonald was often in contact with officials of both the Democratic and Republican Parties, given his stature as a noted historian and a widely respected East Texas leader. *Courtesy Judy McDonald*

McDonald with his longtime administrative assistant, friend, adviser, and, as Ab Abernethy phrased it, "co-conspirator," Portia Gordon. During their work together on behalf of ETHA, Gordon and McDonald provided strong and capable leadership for the organization. *Courtesy Portia Gordon, former administrative assistant to Archie P. McDonald*

The noted folklorist Francis E. "Ab" Abernethy (1925–1915), in the museum-like setting of his office at Stephen F. Austin State University. One of McDonald's dearest friends and closest confidants, Abernethy was the longtime director of the Texas Folklore Society and a strong supporter of ETHA. *Photo courtesy Hardy Meredith, Stephen F. Austin State University*

M. Scott Sosebee, PhD, McDonald's colleague, friend, and successor as executive director of ETHA. *Photo courtesy East Texas Historical Association*

Dan K. Utley and Archie P. McDonald, Round Rock, Texas, 2011. *Courtesy Portia Gordon, former administrative assistant to Archie P. McDonald*

Archie P. McDonald in his office at Stephen F. Austin State University, December 2005. *Courtesy Dr. Allen Richman, Regents Professor, Stephen F. Austin State University, retired*

Archie McDonald hanging up his hat at the start of a Lale Lecture. McDonald's hat was so much a recognizable part of his style, leadership, and presence that when displayed publicly at conferences it signified the meetings were officially under way. Likewise, when he put his hat back on at day's end, the meetings had adjourned. *Courtesy Hardy Meredith, Stephen F. Austin State University*

CHAPTER 5

Gathering with Good Friends

Lucille Terry was a charter member from Jefferson. She was married to a physician named W. S. Terry Jr., who she always called Doctor. He regularly accompanied her to the meetings and was a faithful attendee of the various sessions, although to my knowledge he never presented a paper or reviewed a book. Nevertheless, Doctor would sit dutifully and listen to the presentations, and he probably absorbed more than most because he was quite an intelligent man. Lucille Terry, like Ruth Lester before her, proudly wore the mantle of Jefferson's historical preservationist, which was a distinguished honor in the early days of the Texas preservation movement, where that community set the pace with such projects as the Excelsior Hotel. Both women worked tirelessly to save vestiges of our built environment, and as a result, the highest preservation honor at the Texas Historical Commission is named in honor of Ruth Lester, and the similar honor bestowed by the East Texas Historical Association is named for Lucille Terry.

The ETHA award was Gail Beil's idea, and it followed the precedents set by the board in honoring two previous leaders. The C. K. Chamberlain Award was the first one we ever gave, and that was the brainchild of Joe White. Joe had been a graduate assistant to Dr. Chamberlain. He later taught history at Kilgore College, where he also served as the longtime curator of the magnificent East Texas Oil Museum. The Chamberlain Award honored the best article in a given volume of the journal—two issues together—which was determined by a committee appointed each year by the president. Then we had the Ralph Steen Award, which was to honor the work of people, other than in publishing, to advance the cause of East Texas history through the association. At some point, Gail dutifully noted that our awards were named for men and that there needed to be something named for a woman. Living in Marshall at the time, and thus just sixteen miles from Jefferson, she was aware of the work of Lucille Terry and felt it was worthy of such commemoration. Bob Bowman raised most of the money to endow the award, which is a magnificent piece of sculpture—the logo of the association, in fact—the log cabin come to the third dimension. It is quite solid and weighs a great deal. Bob got an artist named Buck Cheavens to design the sculpture and then contracted with Dell Ray Bronze in Houston to strike the first ten. Together, Bob and Gail helped raise the necessary funds. By the time we ordered our second set of sculptures—at that time and subsequently from Bryant Art Foundry of Azle—Buck Cheavens of Diboll had passed away, so we gave one to his family in his memory. The association also gave one to me when I retired just to get rid of me. All the others, though, have been earned. The Terry Award, coincidentally, does not have a regenerative source of revenue, unlike the others that are funded through an endowment that draws interest. For that reason, we developed a special auction to help raise the necessary support. It is entirely worth the effort; Mrs. Terry was a grand lady, and she was sort of the classic small-community matron beloved by all, and Doctor was always one step behind her, doing whatever she needed.

Another important early leader in the association was Max Lale, who was very special to me. In fact, I keep a picture of him in my office. Max was born in Oklahoma on a truly hardscrabble farm. By sheer brainpower he got into the University of Oklahoma, graduating in the late 1930s. He went through the Reserve Officers Training Corps and was already in the service when World War II started. He was second in command of an artillery regiment and was so good at what he did at Fort Sill that they kept him there as an instructor until the war had advanced a little bit. As a result, he was not involved in the first North African campaign but did get in on everything else in Europe, from Normandy on. He became an executive officer of his artillery division before reaching the rank of lieutenant colonel. When the war was over he came back, intending to be a journalist and writer all along, and he went to work at the *Marshall News Messenger* and there mentored two young men, both of whom ended up working in the White House. They were brothers Bill and James Moyers. Max became the heart and soul of historical-mindedness and preservation in Harrison County. I have no doubt in my mind that the restored courthouse, which is one of the magnificent ones in the state, would never have happened without his persistence. Max was married to a diminutive little woman named Georgiana, who was a sweet lady. I will never forget Bill Moyers's eulogy of her on the *CBS Evening News*, when he was still doing commentary for the network, and his reference to her sewing and being one of the threads that held American communities together. Georgiana stood maybe four and a half feet tall and Max was at least six feet, but they were tight together. Max's journal article "My War" was basically his letters home to her. He later wrote a book by that title about his broadened experiences in the war, but the letters were the source of his remembrances.

Not long after Georgiana died, Max remarried, this time to Georgiana's good friend, Cissy Stewart, who had also worked at the *News Messenger* early in her career. Cissy is from Cleburne and had gone back to that country and was long known as the society columnist for the *Fort Worth Star-Telegram* and was intimate with the Bass family and all the other social leaders in the Fort Worth area. At some point, Max came to me with a proposal for ETHA: "What would you do if I gave you a certain sum of money?" That sum of money turned out to be $30,000. I told him I would start a lecture series, because that was one thing we did not do and was something we could offer to the university in return for what the university does for us—we literally would not be what we are without them. Max thought that was a good idea and it really kind of surprised me then when he said he wanted to name it the "Georgiana and Max S. Lale Series," but he and Cissy had worked that all out. They were really good for each other, and both were active in ETHA in their own way. Max was always interested in history, particularly if it related to Harrison County or Marshall. That was Mecca for him, and everything else was a little less. I remember once at an auction benefiting the Terry Award there was a nondescript box made from a tree cut in Harrison County. He bid well over a hundred dollars for it, but it was made out of Harrison County wood and he was going to take it back home with him to Fort Worth. Although he was from Oklahoma, he fell in love with Marshall.

When I first met Bill Moyers, he was in Marshall to film a piece for his *Walk through the Twentieth Century* television series. He entitled it "Marshall, Texas, Marshall, Texas," and in it, Moyers talked about how he and the civil rights leader James Farmer, the founder of the Congress of Racial Equality, had grown up there at the same time but never knew each other, so segregated was the town. In that piece, part of the film footage had to do with what was declared Max Lale Day.

Another important early member of ETHA was Irvin May. He was from the Overton area, and the main topic he wrote about was the agricultural extension station there, but I first knew him as a faculty member at Texas A&M. He was an agricultural historian, and he involved me in a symposium over there where I delivered a paper called "The Lone Star Brand." I had long been fascinated with the story of M. S. Wright coming to Nacogdoches in 1930. The Depression was just then breaking, and no one in town knew him, but he was a fertilizer salesman who learned that Nacogdoches County's poor old land required more fertilizer than any other. There was no other source locally, so he decided to build a plant. Within less than a week he had borrowed the money and was in business, and the Lone Star plant is still here. Irvin and I just sort of became friends. He eventually moved to Brenham and had a good career at Blinn College. He was a very faithful ETHA member who unfortunately died at a relatively early age. In his will, he remembered the association with a $5,000 bequest, and that was the beginning of our financial foundation that gave us some stability at a time when we measured our expenses in the hundreds of dollars rather than thousands.

In those formative years of the association, membership and financial stability were always concerns. Charter membership in the association because it remained open for a full year after the September 1962 meeting was first listed at more than four hundred, but by the early 1970s it had dwindled to approximately a hundred. I am not sure of all the reasons, but Dr. Steen attributed it in part to the unpredictability of the journal; members never knew exactly when it was coming out, and sometimes the news and announcements had already occurred. But also, I think the newness of the organization had worn off by then. Members had other opportunities, and the meetings we had then only lasted through Saturday mornings. They generally started with a board meeting that might be at seven o'clock, and there might or might not be breakfast, depending on who the president was. There would be a session at nine and then one later in the morning, followed by lunch. After that, everyone went home, so frankly there was not much to attend. Saturdays were our preferred days, because that was when a lot of people could get away from work. In the beginning, there were a lot of members who were teachers, so that worked well. I think the interest just sort of waned and there was not enough programming to keep members interested, which is one of the reasons I called for a Friday afternoon session to bring in more people. I also called for at least two concurrent sessions, which in my mind automatically doubled the number of people who have responsibility and something to do. Now, Francis E. "Ab" Abernethy, director of the Texas Folklore Society (TFS), objected to that, so that group still meets as one body. That is his philosophy, and I am not saying it is wrong, but it worked for us to have multiple sessions and make the meeting longer. Not everybody who comes on Thursday stays until Saturday, and not everybody who is there Saturday came on Thursday, but there is something there for a lot of people all the time, at least within the regularly recognized parameters.

We expanded consciously and purposefully so there would be more activity, more interest, and more participants. The overall change was not immediate, but gradually membership began to grow. The lowest attendance I ever had at a board meeting was my first one in Commerce, and those attending included the president, who was Ralph Goodwin, me, and Tommie Jan Lowery, our treasurer. That was it. The lowest attendance at a spring meeting was twenty-five, and that was in Tyler in the mid-1970s when we were still doing the Saturday morning—only programming. We probably would have had fifty in attendance, but there was a hell of a storm that went through all of East Texas the night before. Of course we got up in the dark to get up there that morning, since no one thought of spending the night in those days. Twenty-five people ultimately showed up and registered, and that was our lowest number. In the fall, the registration was closer to fifty, and that was also a low turnout. Since we have two meetings a year, the way those work out is interesting, with the fall meetings in Nacogdoches considered *the* ones to attend. That is not to say that the spring meetings in other towns are not significant, but they were just different and generally attracted more of the local members, for good reason.

One of the things I was quick to learn is that if we held our spring meeting in Greenville or Paris or somewhere farther north like that, many of the people from the more southerly areas would not come. Conversely, if we held it in Beaumont, most of the Tyler and Longview people would not be there. Galveston, however, was the exception to the rule. Everybody seemed to come there, and of course the attractions in Galveston are the seafood and the Gulf of Mexico. One year there, Maury Darst served as the program chair. A founder of ETHA, Darst had been a student at SFA and then a long-time teacher at Galveston College. He arranged for the meeting to be held at Guido's restaurant and hotel. We had a big contingent, and on that Saturday we had booked the main dining room for our luncheon. The speaker was to be newspaperman Red Parrish, but he failed to show, thinking the event was on a different date. Although I had a copy of his talk and could have given it, I just decided we would do without, because with everyone looking out to the Gulf waters and enjoying a great meal at Guido's, I thought they would be good and happy. We called off the meeting early so everyone could enjoy the great weather that day, and we never had a complaint. I was never able to convince Darst, though, that no one even missed the talk.

We have had great meetings in Tyler, thanks to folks like Lee Lawrence, Linda Cross, Randy Gilbert, Mrs. Loy Gilbert (Alice), Gene Kirkpatrick, and the Smith County Historical Society. We have also had successful gatherings in Beaumont, where we always had good support from the history faculty at Lamar University—Marion Holt, Ralph Wooster, and others. Although it is where I grew up, Beaumont is not quite like Galveston, because there is not that much eminent water, but they have Spindletop and the Jefferson Theater and other great places to visit. At one meeting, we visited the replica Gladys City site, and the local arrangements committee arranged for the Lucas Gusher to actually gush for us. Now, it was clear water and not oil, but the noise and the rumble really gave us a feeling for what that must have been like.

Some of the meetings in smaller towns have been equally memorable. We had one in San Augustine, thanks to Willie Earl Tindall, where we met in, among other places, several vacant buildings downtown. Early on, we also had a good meeting in Henderson in a restored house near downtown. Another good one was held jointly in Paris and Clarksville, where several of us spent quality tourist time in their restored jail. We had good meetings in Marshall always, thanks to folks like Marjorie Perkins, Audrey Kariel, and Gail Beil. On one occasion, we went to Wiley College to see a play about East Texas that featured excerpted passages of oral histories collected by

SFA professor Bobby Johnson. A meeting in Texarkana probably stretched our boundaries the most, even more than when we gathered in Fort Worth. As part of the Texarkana meeting we traveled over to the restored town of Washington in Arkansas and had an old-fashioned meal in the village. It was a bitterly cold night, and we had buggy ride tours of the complex and, since it was touted as the home of the bowie knife, watched knife-making demonstrations.

Our fall meetings in Nacogdoches have consistently been good draws. In our early years, we met in a few rooms on the SFA campus, but as attendance grew, we moved over to the Fredonia Hotel. Except for a brief stint at the Pallas Hotel when the Fredonia closed temporarily, we remained there for many years. It became our surrogate home, in effect, and we had a marvelous relationship with the hotel during all of my time as director. [Editor's note: The Fredonia Hotel, still open at the time of the interview, closed in November 2013. By the fall of 2015 planning was under way that could lead to the reopening of the establishment.] That was largely because the reopening of the Fredonia was a community effort in a way, but it is also due to the leadership of some of Nacogdoches's wealthier people who formed a management company. There were more than twenty key financial backers at one time, but it ultimately boiled down to three: A. T. Mast Jr., Joe Max Green, and a man named Ed Cole. Their vision, generosity, and community spirit kept that place open, and they shouldered the financial burden for about twenty years. They had a manager named Jim Broiles, who came to them first as a representative of a management company, and they just hired him away to work for them. He was a great partner for ETHA and always supportive of our conferences. We, of course, filled the hotel and handled all the catering through the business, with one important exception. Early on, Judy and I would host the Friday evening receptions at our house at 1615 Redbud Street. I used to really love it, because I served as the bartender. I can remember one particular little old lady from Henderson who would come up to me and say, "Just a little more scotch, Doctor." As the gathering grew we moved to other venues, but those informal gatherings helped build friendships among the members, with new ones joining the fun each year. Most recently, we have gathered at the convention and visitors bureau facilities on the square in downtown Nacogdoches, and that gives the gathering a strong sense of historical place.

The idea to have two annual meetings—one in the spring and one in the fall—is unique among the state's historical associations. It came about because it was just simply done from the beginning and was well established for several years before I joined the organization. The Texas State Historical Association (TSHA) utilized that structure in the 1960s and 1970s under Joe B. Frantz. There was always the annual meeting in March that more or less connected with Texas Independence Day, but when Frantz was director there was also a fall meeting to "fly the flag" in another locale. They would be half-day meetings, featuring outside speakers and some local participation, but they helped with membership recruitment, especially with those who might not go to Austin, where all the TSHA meetings were held at that time.

One of those regional TSHA meetings is where I reconnected with Johnny Jenkins [John J. Jenkins]. Johnny and I grew up in Beaumont and were both members of the Frank P. Decker Demolay Chapter there, but we went our separate ways—me into teaching at SFA and him into the publishing business in Austin. By the time we caught up at TSHA, I had developed an idea about a biography on William Barret Travis. It is ironic, but he tried to talk me into doing a book about Edward Burleson, which is who he was working on at the time of his tragic death. Ken Kesselus eventually finished that work. I persevered with Travis, though, and when I got the biography done, I traveled to Austin to meet with Jenkins in that "inner sanctum" he had down there. It was like visiting with Napoleon in a sense. Jenkins was a short man, and he had a large, dark mahogany desk—biggest damn desk and chair I had ever seen—and it was up on a pedestal, so when you sat down, you were looking up at him in his massive chair. He was not actually squatted in it—his poker buddies used to call him "Austin Squatty"—but he sat there as a sort of lord and master, and it was just a wonderful thing to remember. In any event, he published my book under the Pemberton Press imprint, and I was grateful for that. When it sold out, he decided not to reprint it, but he was kind enough to release it to me without charge. Ed Eakin picked it up and it is theoretically available by means of print on demand. One thing in particular I remember about Jenkins is that back in the early 1970s, he essentially predicted the general concept of electronic books. He envisioned that the day would come when we would be able to hold a panel in our hands and read as many books as we wanted. Now that is a reality—and a growing trend—and it is something we have to contend with as we think about the future of the journal, for example.

Someone who figured prominently in the formative work of the association was Ottis Lock, a public school teacher in Zavalla, in southern Angelina County. He taught social studies at an earlier part of his career and retained a lifelong interest in East Texas history. He also became a very prominent businessman and political leader. He served in the Texas House of Representatives and in the Senate, where he was in the top leadership. In fact, he was a member of that Lamar Hotel poker game in Houston that has some fame and infamy in Texas politics. Lock never wanted to be more than he was in the Senate. Asked a number of times if he would run for governor, he always declined, claiming that Austin was just not the place he wanted to live; he wanted to be able to come back to East Texas. Lock was also the mentor of Bob Bowman, because his business career was as an executive with the Southland Paper Company, where Bob worked in public relations. Bowman and Lock were close and developed a mentoring friendship something like a father-son relationship. Years after Lock's death, Bowman wanted to honor his friend and thus arranged for the monies to establish the Ottis Lock Endowment. Some of the funds came from the family and the Pineywoods Foundation, which was a successor to the Kurth Foundation in Lufkin—Ernest L. Kurth being a founder of Southland Paper. We established the endowment to honor various things that historians do in East Texas. There was, for example, in the beginning, an annual award for superior teaching at the secondary and collegiate levels, and other awards for books and articles. There were always research grants to help encourage the work of historians. What has been impressive to me in the grant applications is that in the beginning they were almost exclusively from East Texans for East Texas projects, and obviously that's part of the criteria. In later years, though, the applications have come from places like Virginia, New Jersey, and various other out-of-region locales, but of course they all must focus on East Texas. At one time we had a sort of a traveling museum display that included photos of Mr. Lock, his briefcase, a badge he had when he was in public office, and various other things, and that was all constructed for us by Ab Abernethy. In addition to his work as an SFA English professor and the TFS director, he turned into an excellent museum constructionist. He could build a display with the best of them.

Through the years, the ETHA established important relationships with other organizations doing similar work to ours. One early connection in that regard was with the Texas Historical Commission (THC). My first involvement with that agency came as a result of being chair of the Nacogdoches County Historical Survey Committee, as it was called then. That was an appointment made by the county judge simply because I was a historian teaching Texas history; there were no politics involved. I remember attending the annual conference in Waco, which is where I believe I first met the director, Truett Latimer, who was a former member of the Texas Legislature. Later, I was appointed to the THC's State Board of Review, serving two terms. In that capacity, I traveled all over the state to various meetings, sitting somewhat in judgment about whether or not individual sites qualified for the National Register of Historic Places.

Through my association with the THC, I got involved in other statewide activities. I was appointed to a commemorative initiative regarding El Camino Real. The legislature had created a commission to help us remember the tercentennial, the three-hundredth anniversary of the blazing by Spanish provincial governor Domingo Terán de los Ríos of El Camino Real up to East Texas. Because I failed to think fast enough, General John McGifford, who was then running the Texas Institute of Letters, nominated me to be chairman of the project. Nancy Kenmotsu, who was a THC archaeologist, served as a statutory member of the Tercentennial Commission, which had an office at the THC. Others with statutory roles included the Texas Parks and Wildlife Department and the Texas Department of Transportation, which also had a team of archaeologists working with us. Al McGraw comes to mind in that regard, and the result of all the archaeological research was a study that I believe definitively identified the various trails collectively known as El Camino Real.

By that time, the new THC director was Curtis Tunnell, himself an archaeologist, and I also worked closely with Barney Davis, of Somerville, then the chairman of the historical commission. Incidentally, when Latimer left the agency in the early 1980s, someone invited me to apply for the agency directorship, but I was pretty well cemented at SFA. The commission, though, made the ideal appointment in Curtis Tunnell. He was the right person for that job, and he kept it a long time and did great work. I was fortunate later to be appointed by Governor Ann Richards to be a commissioner and to eventually serve as vice chairman for my last two years of service. I only served one term, because I was appointed by a Democrat, and the next governor, George W. Bush, was a Republican. I understood the game and I never held that against Governor Bush for not reappointing me, although I admit I tried to be reappointed, because I wanted to serve again.

Our work with the THC and other agencies and associations reflected the structure of a broader historical community in a definable way. Those of us active in the history field in the state came to know each other because we had contact on various levels of our work. If you look at the founders of our association, Ruth Lester was the moving force in the state preservation movement and with the organization of the historically minded people in Jefferson. Max Lale, although he was not technically a founder, was similarly involved in Marshall with the Harrison County Historical Commission. Lee Lawrence in Tyler was the heart and soul of the Smith County Historical Society, which in my judgment was at one point the most active county or regional historical society in the state. There were other local historians who come to mind, including Eliza Honey Bishop of Houston County, specifically Crockett. There was also an active group in Beaumont called the Gulf Coast Historical Society. Peter Wells, an attorney in Beaumont, was a real authority on everything connected with the Texas Navy, and he was an active member of ETHA. Mostly, though, the support in the Beaumont area came from the Lamar University faculty. In the beginning it was Ralph Wooster and Preston Williams, who was the chairman of the History Department, and in later years there was Jo Ann Stiles and now Mary Kelley-Scheer. There were, regrettably, gaps in the membership, like in the Big Thicket counties of Jasper, Hardin, and Tyler, and it was kind of like we jumped over the Thicket to get to the Gulf Coast.

When I think of the state and national heritage organizations that occasionally worked with us, there were never any official partnerships. To borrow a line from Al Lowman, the people who were interested in that sort of thing were interested in that sort of thing. One of my cherished book review lines came from Lowman, who found himself with nothing really negative to say about a particular book, but with nothing positive to mention either, so he concluded by simply noting, "those who like this sort of book will like this sort of book," which is exquisite double-talk. But many of our members, like Ruth Lester for example, were active in the major heritage organizations. Carolyn Ericson, who is a strong member of our association from Nacogdoches and a frequent book exhibitor at our meetings, is also active in those groups, like the United Daughters of the Confederacy, the Daughters of the Republic of Texas, and the Daughters of the American Revolution. Yet Carolyn is interested in East Texas history for reasons far beyond genealogy and bookselling.

Another of those associations with historical groups that comes to mind involved the Texas Sesquicentennial Commission, which operated under legislative mandate in the 1980s to commemorate the 150th anniversary of the Declaration of Independence from Mexico. Originally, the statutory membership did not include any private historical organizations other than TSHA, so I approached our state senator, Roy Blake, about the discrepancy. I knew Blake very well, and my wife was his campaign manager for his last two elections. I just told him I thought East Texas should be represented. Well, he hemmed and hawed a little bit, and finally he said, "You just want me to change the law." And I said, "Well, I suppose that's exactly what I want you to do," and he said "Huh," and then added, "Well okay, it might be fun." The Texas Speaker of the House at that time was Billy Clayton. Roy and Billy were close friends, so he went to Billy and said, "I want to change this and I want to add this East Texas Historical Association representative to the commission." Well, Clayton was a West Texan, so he said, "If we're going to do that, we're going to add the West Texas Historical Association (WTHA)." The WTHA at that time was run by B. W. Aston, but he was never terribly interested in the position for some reason, so Alwyn Barr of Texas Tech became the WTHA member and I represented the ETHA on the Sesquicentennial Commission.

Now, as luck would have it, my time as president of the Texas State Historical Association coincided with the Sesquicentennial, so I was the ETHA director, I was a member of the Sesquicentennial Commission, and then I was president of TSHA from March 1985 to March 1986. When the commemoration was really buzzing, TSHA had a great big birthday bash for the state. I remember leading the singing of "Texas, Our Texas," and they had a cake as big as a desk, and everybody got a slice of it, and the whole meeting was focused around the Sesquicentennial. At least for that one moment we were all together. Even ETHA members who had not been active in TSHA were there, and we were all in as one for the big blowout, and we had a good time.

The relationship between the WTHA and the ETHA has historically been an interesting one. They are a bit older than the first iteration of our association, but in the early days of both organizations there was not much opportunity for overlap, because there was not as much regional travel as there is today. However, a lot of East Texans went out there to hunt, because the trees are not in the way to shoot deer, so they grew to appreciate that region. In any event, I do not know that we had but a handful maybe of our members who were also members of WTHA. Over the years, though, we came to know each other through TSHA and other groups, so at some point their director, Tai Kreidler, and I began discussing the possibility of some joint sessions. This was common then at TSHA meetings, which had sessions from the TFS, the THC, the Texas Catholic Historical Society, and many others. So we started doing that about fifteen years ago, and if memory serves, we hosted the first one, which included Judge Tom Crum, of Granbury, who has subsequently served as president of both organizations. When Tom was president of the WTHA, I was also invited to be the banquet speaker in Lubbock. It has been a successful endeavor through the years, and I am absolutely confident it has benefited and enriched both organizations.

Although it was not an official connection, we also worked with the Civil War Round Tables. We operated one locally for a while that primarily involved people from Nacogdoches and Angelina Counties, and we administered it out of our office. I remember in particular working with attorney Cooper Reagan, one of our charter members who also headed the Houston Civil War Round Table, one of the earliest. Of course, the first was in Chicago in the 1940s. It grew out of Ralph Newman's Abraham Lincoln Book Shop, on Chestnut Street, where Civil War buffs would hang around to talk history. That led to the gatherings becoming more institutionalized. Cooper Reagan, by the way, had served as attorney to the noted Texas lumberman John Henry Kirby. He was one of the last professional southerners in a way and had a magnificent Texana collection. He had a house in River Oaks in Houston, and when I first met him I was a student at Rice. Reagan and my professor, Frank Vandiver, were cofounders of the Jefferson Davis Papers Association, which headquartered there.

Another good friend of ETHA that comes to mind is Willie Earl Tindall, one of the saints of this earth. When I first came to SFA, she was working in the Boynton Library on the campus. She was from San Augustine, Texas, and was married to that town's famous sheriff, Nathan Tindall, who was probably as close to a John Wayne incarnate in law enforcement as I have ever been privileged to know. He was the "high sheriff," and he worried a whole lot more about justice than he did about the law. In any event, Willie Earl took me under her wing as it were, even though we were close to the same age. That made it possible for me to mine that library, as much as it had in it, and would do all kinds of things to facilitate my research. She became the heart and soul of the historical community of San Augustine. She also served on our board, and if there was ever a financial need that was not too extravagant, Willie Earl would quietly take care of it, never wanting any recognition. When we lost our storage here on the campus one time, she let us use a room in the alternative school that she operated for the San Augustine School District. She put a lock on the door, and she and I were the only ones with keys. I guess the district officials knew they were providing the space, but whether they did or not, the arrangement continued until Willie Earl passed away. Even then, they let us stay. At some point, though, we figured it was a good time to retrieve everything. A graduate student named Dyson Nickle had a big horse trailer, which he cleaned out thoroughly for us, and we went over there and got all of our stuff and brought it back over here.

Another member who did so much to professionalize the organization was Kenneth Hendrickson, a West Texan who taught for many years at Midwestern State University in Wichita Falls. I met Ken largely through Ben Procter at TSHA, but I also saw him at the Southern Historical Association meetings. We were always going together to dinner with Ben, and then for years we did an annual presentation at a Catholic school in Dallas, and we became really, really close friends. I am flattered to think that Ken's intense involvement with us was largely a consequence of our friendship. He would always make the extra effort to come to our meeting when he could not always attend others, but he was that interested. It is a long drive from Wichita Falls to come to one of our meetings, and I am sure it felt twice as long going home afterward, but he did it for many years.

Although Ben Procter, of TCU, never figured as prominently in ETHA as Ken did, he was nevertheless important to me personally. He has been the closest person to me over the longest period of time in the historical profession in Texas. For him and Lee Lawrence, I cannot exaggerate how much I owe the two of them in terms of what little dent I have made in

Texas history studies. It was Lee working through Ben, then chairman of the TSHA nominating committee, who got me on the board. Lee believed strongly there should be an East Texan on the TSHA board. Although he believed they strove to be balanced, he also perceived a slight slant toward the western traditions, so he asked Ben to work to get me on the council. I did not know Ben at that time, so I met up with him in Fort Worth. He was in his Kojak period then, bald headed and walking around sucking on a Tootsie Roll sucker. We got into his oversize car—Ben has always driven big cars because he is a big man—and we drove around maybe a couple of hours with him sort of interrogating and interviewing me, but apparently I passed. He could be intimidating, because he was a very intense person, particularly if something was compelling his interest. Once I passed muster, though, they put me on the council and Ben and I became partners in the politics of TSHA for the next decade or so.

We also served together on the THC's Board of Review and nearly precipitated a riot in Houston one time. The issue primarily was consideration of the National Register designation for a local neighborhood known as the Fourth Ward, a predominantly African American area. A lot of the landowners, many of them absentee, were worried about any type of federal intervention, and developers and city planners were also interested in the land for other reasons, so there was plenty of tension, as well as media presence. Ben and I developed our strategy to deal with the matter, and when one of us made the motion to approve the historical designation, the other one immediately pounced on the second, and we went straight to a vote. It happened so fast the camera crews missed it all.

The association made a lot of strong connections through the years in all parts of the state, but we always had to remember who we truly represented. As part of our outreach to the various communities we serve, and in an effort to celebrate our past, we started writing a series of newspaper articles on East Texas. The effort began as a grant-funded project to tell the history of Nacogdoches County, but over time it grew. In 2000, Bob Bowman and I expanded the project to include all of East Texas, and we produced regular articles under the banner "All Things Historical." The point was to offer them free to East Texas newspapers, but of course that was free publicity for us as well. Through his public relations work and his earlier experience publishing a Diboll newspaper, Bowman knew most of the editors, so it worked well. We produced an article every two weeks, and I believe at one point we were in as many as fifty weeklies and dailies. In a similar vein, we would also occasionally make presentations in various parts of East Texas to promote regional history and our association. To assist in that endeavor, we produced a video about the association and its various programs; Bowman wrote the script, and a local radio personality, Bob Dunn, provided the narration. Mark Barringer, Portia Gordon, her husband, Charlie, and I made several of those barnstorming trips throughout to recruit new members. Another part of our outreach involved a series of topical symposia, like on civil rights and on the Toledo Bend area, that proved very successful and that allowed us to focus on a wide variety of regional history.

While we made good strides in promoting and celebrating our history through the years, eventually growing to more than six hundred members, it was due in large part to the interests of our members—our friends. There was no master plan. It was just like a ball coming down through a pinball machine, bouncing off things and, for the most part, bouncing true. We had some failures, too, but for the most part, it turned out pretty good.

CHAPTER 6

The Best

Through SFA, we always had a good group of office assistants who came from the student ranks. I remember such folks as Dyson Nickle, Dennis Bradford, Ron Spiller, Chris Spaid, and Linda Hudson, who later became president of ETHA. Linda was from the Longview area and was interested in all aspects of East Texas history. I believe I first met her when she showed up at an ETHA meeting in Lufkin, but then later, as an SFA student, she started working in the association office. What I remember most is directing her academic thesis on the Knights of the Golden Circle, which was a topic I alerted her to. At the completion of her master's work, I recommended she go to TCU and in fact took her up to TCU and visited with my friend Ben Procter, but she elected instead to go to the University of North Texas and work with Mike Campbell. He is the one who put her on to the Jane Cazneau topic, which led to her significant book entitled *Mistress of Manifest Destiny*. When Linda Hudson became the ETHA president, she and other members worked to start a women's breakfast session at our conferences. She later wrote a journal article about her experiences in that regard, in which she said I growled and summoned and did all kinds of other things with regard to trying to block it, but actually I was doing my damnedest to facilitate the idea. What she and others never knew was that I was getting considerable resistance from some longtime members who thought it would be divisive. I had seen it work in the Southern Historical Association and other groups, so I was not afraid of it in that way, but there was still resistance. Sometimes it is hard to calculate when you offend someone, particularly someone who is supporting the organization in a fiduciary way. You just have to be cautious. In this case, I was the meat in the sandwich—the two sides wanted it to go their particular ways, and I wanted it to go a certain way, but at the same time I had to honor the other people who were important to the association. Obviously, it did not turn out to be all that divisive, because it is still going on. Later we added another breakfast meeting regarding African American history, thanks to the work of Ted Lawe of Emory and Dallas. It was certainly through his influence and labor that it got started well, and he was backed in those efforts by ETHA staff members Mark Barringer and Scott Sosebee. It, too, resulted in a nice added dimension.

In both instances, though, from the beginning, I said we would be glad to make the arrangements and collect the meal fees, but we could not assume responsibility for the programs. The interest groups themselves had to do that, and they have succeeded. When the women's breakfast started, some members were upset I did not attend, but that early-morning time was particularly busy for me. They would meet around seven thirty in the morning, which was when I was making sure everything else was going to work just thirty minutes later. I had no time to add anything extra. When we started a conference, it was showtime for me. As director, I was on duty twenty-four hours a day from the Wednesday before the meetings began until late Saturday afternoon when it was all over. I would meet up with my assistant, Portia Gordon, by eight, even though the meeting did not officially start until later, and we would make sure the board room was set up right and all the things that we brought to the meeting were available. We also had to make sure the registration was ready to go, because she literally had no time—not even for lunch sometimes—to go from the board meeting straight into the registration. The attendees expect personal attention, and they deserve it. Most of them are members, and they have showed up and paid their money, and they need to be accommodated. But they could also be early, you know. We would often have people lined up in the hotel lobby wanting to register before we went into the board meeting, and that made it difficult. Mrs. Gordon handled it well, utilizing preregistrations, but there were always folks who showed up to register that day, and that just took time. She always seemed to have the patience it took. She had a fantastic memory for names, and not just of the members, but their kids as well. She even remembered the members' illnesses and would inquire about their health. It was a huge asset for the association. In my case, there were always people who wanted some part of my time to ask for a book to review, to pitch an article, or to request a place on the program. There were always some for whom such exchanges were not one-time contacts; seemingly, every time I turned around there were always two or three, and this was constantly going on the whole three days.

In terms of the leadership of the association, I need to give credit to the Fellows. The designation of Fellows came before the Steen Award, which was for service to the association other than writing. The Fellows, though, was specifically for those who demonstrated scholarship through publications. In the beginning there were people on the Fellows list who may or may not ever come to a meeting, but they had written something significant on the history of Texas. I think we started out with a limit of twenty-five, whereas TSHA had fifty at the time, so that is appropriate. I may be mistaken on this, but I think it was my idea to have a Fellows designation. It was not exactly a copycat of TSHA, but I recognized that it was a meaningful designation to that particular organization and presumed it was to others, so I wanted to create that kind of, let's say, fellowship here with the association. And if it was not my idea, it ought to have been. Anyway, that was my reasoning about it that we should honor those who had been significant writers, and the list changes as each passing of a Fellow creates a new vacancy. I was a member of that first class in 1982, joined by Randolph "Mike" Campbell, Robert S. Maxwell, and J. Milton Nance. If I could have influenced that decision—because this is the way I operate—I would not have let them do that for me the very first year. Sometimes I could not avoid things that people wanted to do for me. Additionally, with but one exception, I also never agreed to be on the programs at the association meetings while I was director. The only time I agreed was when Linda Cross asked me to do a musical number. I could not say no to her, so I agreed.

Linda Cross taught at Tyler Junior College and had been a student of mine at SFA. She was an undergraduate student first, and at that time she was pregnant. I mean, she was enormous to the point where I asked her, "Linda, when *was* this baby going to be born?" I knew the date of the final exam, and the due date was a little before that, so I said, "You're going to have to tell me what to do." When my two sons were born, everything was on time and orderly, so I had no experience otherwise. I needed her to tell me what to do in the case of an emergency. Now this is pretty damn bold for a professor in the 1960s to be talking to a female student like that. Well, fortunately, an emergency arose when she was not at school, but you know, I swear I don't think she missed but one class.

Despite that one speaking exception for Linda, I declined such invitations, because it was just not right for me to take up space. That is a lesson I learned when I was president of TSHA. That year I obviously had to deliver the presidential address, but other folks I had difficulty saying no to asked me to do a morning session with J. P. Bryan. I was to talk on William Travis and his topic was Stephen F. Austin. The session was very well attended, there is no question of that, but they were all there to hear J. P., I'm sure. When it was over, though, I still had a full day of Sesquicentennial events followed by my presidential speech. I was beat. I stayed up late after the dinner; they gave a reception, and a bunch of people came to Austin, so I had to be congenial, but that was just one log too many on the load. That was just part of the reasoning for begging off on program requests for ETHA. The main reason was I just never thought it was proper for the hired help to take up space that the volunteers could have used. That was my attitude with regard to the awards and the structure of the awards, and so forth. I remember once *Texas Monthly* gave TSHA one of its Bum Steer Awards for giving itself a book award for the revised *Handbook of Texas*. You know, I don't think anybody in the world who understood Texas history would have questioned that that was the best book on Texas history published that year, and that was the criterion of the award, but it just did not wash.

For ETHA, we had a structured format for our leadership. Normally, to be president of the organization, one had to serve awhile on the board of directors. After serving for a term or two, an individual might be asked to serve in the rotation for leadership of the organization, first as second vice president, then first vice president, and then finally president. I set up the rotation system so the second vice president always chaired the membership committee, and the point was that the individual could build the organization he or she would later serve as president. Then the first vice president always chaired the program committee for the fall meeting, which would also be the meeting where they became president. My rationale was that the incoming president could stage the biggest extravaganza they wanted for the time when they would be riding the top of the wave. Then, after a yearlong term as the leader, the past president would serve on the board of directors for another two years for the sake of continuity.

We have been fortunate to have effective presidents through the years. The first two, Lee Lawrence and F. I. Tucker, were both founders, and as such, they were critical to the early development of the association. Lee, by the way, remained on the board until his death. Some way or another, he was just always there, so finally we institutionalized his presence by making him a permanent board member. He was not just the father, he was the shepherd in a great many ways, and he kept us going. Bob Glover was the fourth president and was also an early strong supporter. He was the first chair of the Lucille Terry Award Committee and kept that position for ten years, and really got that program off the ground and going. Ralph Wooster, who was the seventh president, is the surviving charter member of the association so far as I know. He is still a member and has always been supportive of the association. I think every year that I was director he would send an undesignated check for us to use for whatever we needed. In the early days especially, it was timely when that check arrived. Another early president was James L. Nichols, who was a professor at SFA, and it was during his presidency that I became the director. Nichols was a distinguished Civil War scholar in his own right, and maybe the most educated, learned man on the war other than Frank Vandiver, although he did not publish much. In World War II, Nichols was an engineer and went ashore at Normandy in the fourth wave or so. Following him as president was Robert Cotner, from the University of Texas, who was a biographer of James Stephen Hogg and an old-school man in very many ways. During his presidency, I asked the board for allowance to set up a ten-dollar petty cash fund in the office to buy postage or other necessities to operate on, and you would have thought I was asking for the US treasury. That response came from a generation of people who went through the Great Depression and who may have seen instances of fiduciary laxity or chicanery, or where trust of that nature had been violated. One thing I learned early on, though, was never to handle money directly. It always went through my secretary, who after a while was also the association treasurer. Occasionally, people would hand me money, and when they did I never put it in my pocket. I would place it in a folder or it would stay in my hand until I could give it personally to the treasurer, and everybody could see the transfer. I never wanted anybody to wonder about where their cash went. The only checks I ever signed the whole time were to the person who signed the checks—the secretary—because we sometimes had to compensate that individual for expenses. I never ever signed a check for which I was the beneficiary, but I always signed a check if it was to the secretary's benefit, because it was just not proper for the person receiving the check to also sign it, and it is not good business. That was the way we operated, but I remember that Cotner was afraid—and it really was insulting—that a petty cash fund could lead to problems, like somehow that ten dollars would corrupt the staff. Those were different times for sure.

Maury Darst, I remember, was president in 1974–1975. He had lived in Nacogdoches and he loved the town, but he taught in Galveston and was a very good teacher, as I remember. Then Ralph Steen stepped in to become president after not having gone through all the other preliminaries, because Mrs. E. H. Lassiter from Henderson declined to become president after serving as first vice president. I was never sure of her reasoning in that regard, but the closer she got to the presidency, it turned out to be something she did not want to do. Steen had just retired as president of SFA and I was in a bind, so I went to him and asked if he would just step straight in as president. He was the appropriate person because he had been in at the beginning and kept up with it all along. Not only that, but of all the people I ever worked with, he knew how to be a president. He was a good one.

A later president was Frank Smyrl, who went to the University of Oklahoma and became dean at the University of Texas at Tyler. It was under Smyrl's presidency that the title of director was added to my job; I was called the editor up until then. Even though I had a new title, nothing really changed, because I was doing the same things before and after. It was Bobby Johnson's influence that got that done. He knew Smyrl, and he recommended the title change, which added prestige to the position, and sometimes that is crucial when the director is dealing with presses and editors or with others doing business with the association.

Another significant president was Marion Holt, from Beaumont, who was a strong leader of the organization. Bill Brophy was my best friend here on the campus, and when he stepped in as president he was everything administratively. He was the chair of the SFA History Department. He also served as dean and was an interim president at SFA for eight months, but he took time out to be president of the association at a pretty crucial phase.

It was in 1984 and 1985, when I was extremely busy with my TSHA leadership duties. I was fortunate—and maybe unfortunate to a degree—that much of the time a historian was president of SFA. On the one hand, I couldn't fool them, because they knew what historians were supposed to do, but it was ultimately fortunate, because regardless of their field, they were involved with professional associations. I don't think that ever resulted in any great cornucopia of blessings from the administration financially, but it always made it relatively smooth. But even when the presidents or president were not historians, Bill Brophy was almost always in the administration and would kind of look out for the association and for me, and it never hurts to have a friend in court.

Then there was Bob Bowman who was an important supporter of the association for a good many years. He created the Best of East Texas Award and the Lock Awards, and he raised most of the money for the Terry Award. The Pineywoods Foundation that Bowman headed was a source of the sponsorship for at least half of the symposia we held, particularly in the late twentieth century and the first part of the twenty-first century. We were close friends; we probably had lunch together twice a month, and we both also served on the Texas Sesquicentennial Commission. For those meetings we would usually drive back and forth to Austin together, obviously for the companionship as well as the sharing of costs. Briefly we also served on the Red River Radio Board Committee until he decided his business demanded much more of his time. We served together on the Texas Committee for the Humanities, and in fact he succeeded me as president there. He later also served on the Texas Historical Commission after I was not there, so we had a lot in common and were good friends, and I believe that was beneficial to the association for a great part of that time.

Joe White, president in 1984–1985, was a graduate student at SFA in 1964, when I showed up, and has been a member of the Lock Committee since the beginning. He presently runs the East Texas Oil Museum at Kilgore College and has served on the city council, and is quite active in that community. He was the originator of the idea for the Chamberlain Award and raised the initial endowment. Others have contributed to it since, but Joe was the one who got it started because he wanted to honor Chamberlain, for whom he was a graduate assistant, and for whom he also worked on the journal. Another president from Kilgore was Virginia Long, who served 1987–1988.

Through the Long Foundation, she was sometimes an important financial resource for us. She was always interested in what we were doing and occasionally would just send a check. Like Bowman and me, she also served on the Texas Historical Commission. Linda Cross, who I mentioned earlier as a student of mine, also served as president. Then later came Bill O'Neal, who is a strong supporter. He is at every meeting and never turned me down on any request I made of him. He would regularly attend the fall meeting but would leave on Friday afternoon to broadcast his hometown football games in the evening. He was the voice of the Carthage Bulldogs. He is a fine historian of many interests, from the Old West gunfighters to the Civil War, and even baseball. It was to him that I turned when we started the publication series that Bob Bowman financed. Bill did the first book in that effort, which was *War in East Texas: Regulators vs. Moderators.* I suggested the topic and Bill just ran with it and produced a magnificent study. It is the essential source on the topic that everybody else is going to have to consult. He is on the Lock Committee and has probably served as program committee chair for the spring meetings more than anyone else.

While on the topic of presidents, I need to mention Patricia Kell. I have known Pat since 1957, when Judy and I married in Beaumont. We moved into a fourplex—in actuality a big old house that had two apartments upstairs and two apartments downstairs, with shared entrances in the back. Pat and her husband, Eddie, lived next door to us when we were newlyweds. She was from Missouri but took to Texas like a duck to water. She was for many years the curriculum coordinator in the Baytown school system and was the key person in the association for developing the website. I will admit to a little foot dragging on that, because I never fully understood computers and websites, and those types of things. It was out of ignorance that I failed to proceed more rapidly than I did when she brought up the topic, but she was persistent and we finally did get one going. R. G. Dean, who later served as president, set the first one up for us.

Later presidents were Linda Hudson, who I have mentioned, and Ken Hendrickson of Midwestern State University. Ken and I were close friends from a number of other associations, so he started coming to our meetings, and that was a long haul from Wichita Falls. He was a good president—he's forceful. I always called him the "Marlboro Man" because he had that look to me. He was not one to wear cowboy boots or other trappings, though, and he is not a Texan; he is from the Midwest. He was big and brawny and had a stern look on his face all the time, and he could be kind of intimidating to those who didn't know him well. He is a great guy, though.

Gail Beil, of course, I must mention. Gail is a force all by herself and came to us I think largely through Max Lale, as she was a self-appointed caretaker for Max and Georgiana and then later Max and Cissy. Gail was the one who had the idea for the Terry Award to recognize outstanding historical preservation in our region. Certainly that is one of the key charges from our founding, so I was glad we added it and named it for Lucille Terry, which is appropriate. Interestingly, one thing we ask of the recipients is that the award be displayed publicly. It is good publicity for that organization, as well as for ETHA.

Cary Wintz, a longtime professor at Texas Southern University, was a relatively recent president of significance, and he did a lot of work for the association and made us more conscious of the African American part of our East Texas heritage. His book *Black Dixie* is a standard in Texas history. Then we had this guy Dan K. Utley, and I really am not sure what to make of him. He was our only president I worked with who never presided over the program or gave his presidential address, because he had the "gall" to say he was in the hospital somewhere. But he did have the forethought to have his friend Cynthia Beeman read the address for us, and then we were in communication with him via telephone throughout the meeting telling him of some untoward events, as well as some successful things that were going on. He was an excellent president and a good friend, and in fact he's running this oral history operation today.

I want to be sure to mention Beverly Rowe, because she is a lady of steel. I know one other woman, and I can at this point appropriately say intimately, who has been severally blessed with an iron will, and that of course would be my wife. I was not necessarily astonished, but pleasantly surprised, to discover that trait in Beverly, because she is so quiet. She has such an unassuming way about her. She could drift into a circle and you might not notice it because she may not say much when she shows up there, and when she does say something, it is so softly spoken you almost have to lean forward to hear it. But when it came to decision time, she was right up there with Harry Truman. I would say in one way, the association owes maybe its continued existence to her and her resolution to approach problems and deal with them. Milton Jordan took over at a good time and was a great president—a fantastic president. I guess retired preachers know how to deal with all kinds of elements, and he did a really good job. I also want to commend Ted Lawe, who was Milton's predecessor. Ted was our first African American president, and he is very interested in making African American history a legitimate part of our history, which, of course, it should be. He would not necessarily point to what was left out of the story, but he made sure to add other parts in. He reminds me in a way of C. L. Simon, who served with my wife, Judy, on the city commission here in Nacogdoches. There is no doubt in my mind that Simon would have been the local school superintendent had he not been African American. When the schools merged, he was the principal of the African American high school, so he became the assistant principal of the integrated high school. He ultimately became head of personnel for the district, and he was a wonderful man. I've often said of C. L., he accomplished infinitely more on the city commission and in his jobs with the schools for African American education and African American representation with quiet dignity than he ever could have with strident protest. Now, there is a place for strident protesters, because sometimes, particularly back in the fifties and sixties, had there not been people like Martin Luther King Jr. and James Farmer, and even Stokely Carmichael, the ball never would have advanced down the field, I'm confident of that. Ted Lawe reminds me of C. L. Simon, because he is such a fine gentleman and a gregarious fellow, and he was a good president.

Although I obviously never served as president of ETHA, what I observed in others who had that assignment through the years served me well when I became president of TSHA in the spring of 1985. Tuffly Ellis was the director then, having succeeded Joe B. Frantz. Through my extended work on the council, I had worked first with Frantz as director and been much involved in the selection of his successor. Tuffly then did that job for about a decade but then decided to resign. Three days after I was installed as president, I got the letter of his resignation in which he, in effect, said he had been waiting for me to become president because he wanted the transition to occur during the leadership of an academic. He recommended three members of a search committee for his successor, and all of them were from Austin. I knew immediately that was not going to work and that I had to get somebody outside of the capital city to go with them. When I talked to Bob King, who was the dean at the University of Texas with oversight of the association, he told me in no uncertain terms he would not work with one of those members, so obviously I had to find a replacement. Two members I appointed to the committee were absolutely essential to the success of the effort, and I could not have done without them. They were my friends Ben Procter and Lee Lawrence, who were the two leaders of the main camps in the organization. TSHA, to a much greater degree than ETHA, has a division of leadership among the lay members and the academic members. Lee was the leader of the lays and Ben of the academics, and fortunately they were good friends; otherwise I think the organization would have split. But I knew darned good and well I had to have them involved, and so I appointed them. They quickly set about their work.

Tuffly had made arrangements for Jim Pohl at Southwest Texas State University to become the interim director for a year. Before the year was over, though, I suggested we just keep Jim. Now, Jim Pohl would have been the first person to tell you he was not a Texas historian; he was instead a military historian, and a darned good one, and he had served as an officer in combat during the Korean Conflict. He was an excellent historian in every respect, and a great cartoonist, by the way. He used to draw the most unflattering pictures of me in meetings, and they are in my papers at SFA. Ultimately, I guess Jim just wanted to stay in San Marcos, which is close to Austin, but in any event we had to look elsewhere. As the committee made progress in that search, I received a letter, and it was probably from Ben, asking me to apply for the directorship. Now, without attempting to slight ETHA—and let me say up front, I'm glad it worked out so I could finish my career with the association and with Stephen F. Austin State University—but if I can be a little bit presumptuous here, I am probably a little bit bigger frog in this pond than I would have been in that Austin pond—a great deal. But that's not the reason I stayed. I considered it, of course, and was extremely flattered, because for a person who wrote and taught Texas history and worked with associational aspects of that history, there was no better promotion at that time. But there were two things wrong with it and they both had to do with timing. One, I had appointed the committee, and my response to whoever wrote me the letter was that it just would not be proper and would not, in effect, pass the smell test. I never in my appointment of the committee members intimated, nor did it even cross my mind, that

I would be the next director. But more importantly than that, Judy had served ten years on the city commission here, the last half of that more or less understood in tutorage to become the next mayor. A. L. Mangham was the mayor then and a good friend of ours and had said, more or less, that when he quit, he wanted Judy to be his successor. He had been mayor for thirteen years. I thought he would have stopped the time before, in which case she would have already been mayor, but he chose to run one more term. But regardless, she was poised to become mayor of Nacogdoches and I could not disrupt that, especially after I had "gigolo-ed" my way through two graduate schools with her working and putting up with God knows what. Everything we have become professionally was enabled by her sacrifice for my education, and raising babies and all that other kind of stuff, and then going back into a life that was doing an awful lot of good for a lot of people. The legacy goes on; I mean, she has been out of office for more than ten years and there are still people in the African American community here who will call her mayor when they see her. There are professionals, particularly women, who will say, "You visited my elementary school and you are part of why I am now a doctor," or why I am now this, that, or another. I could not take her away from that, and I sure as hell was not going to live in Austin with her over here, so I just said no, because there were too many negatives and not enough positives. In the end it worked out wonderfully, because the UT-TSHA relationship, often fraught with politics, turned sour later on, so I would have been gone a long time before. Once I made the decision, I never looked back. I never one time regretted it.

So, I stayed with ETHA and SFA, and I enjoyed what I was doing. I likened what we were doing to that biblical picking up of the calf. We started doing so little and we ended up doing a great deal, but it was incremental, and I developed the ability to at least muddle through. I will leave it to others' judgment whether or not it was successful. I could not have done it, let me hasten to add, without the assistance of a wonderful secretary, Mrs. Portia Gordon, who could run the association by herself, frankly.

Mrs. Gordon came to us when we had an unexpected opening, and at the time I was traveling quite a bit grading exams for the Advanced Placement Program out of Princeton. I had been doing it since they were quartered in New Jersey. I then followed them from there to Clemson and on to Trinity University in San Antonio. It was a very structured program; I mean, we would go to work at eight in the morning, have a fifteen-minute break in the midmorning, take an hour for lunch, have another fifteen-minute break in the afternoon, and then get off at five. It would be that way five days or more in a row, and if you were a table leader, which I eventually was, you added two or three days to that because you had to get there early for prep. Although the schedule was tight, the Princeton folks nonetheless were quite generous to me at times, allowing me to leave New Jersey at one point to go over to be on the television show *CBS This Morning* to talk about one of my books, *Helpful Cooking Hints for HouseHusbands of Uppity Women*. They also let me go to Austin one time for a program on the history of the Governor's Mansion recorded by the History Channel. *Castles* was the name of the program.

During all that, we needed a new secretary, so Portia just applied. She was a captive. By that I mean she had a husband, Charlie, who was working in Lufkin, and they decided to live in Nacogdoches. They were from farther up in East Texas and had lived for about twenty years in Diana, in Upshur County. Once they moved to Nacogdoches, she went through the human resources office at the university and applied for our job. She had good work skills and was mature (not old) and settled, and she had an infectious smile. She was always aware of the work we needed done, and she was friendly and open, and we have worked marvelously together all these years, and Judy and Charlie are good friends, too.

After many years as an effective team, though, the time came to talk about my retirement. At SFA, we had enjoyed relatively remarkable stability in our administration, from Ralph Steen and Bill Johnson to Bill Brophy, who was interim, and many others who became friends. I also had a number of liberal arts deans who were close friends during those years as well, including Jim Reese, another historian. They always appreciated the association, and they always knew what I was doing, and if there was something they wanted to know, they would ask me and I would give them the information, so we got along really well. Then there came a dramatic change in leadership, with a new president, provost, and dean named in short order. With that change there were also new directions for some of the programs outside the History Department, including ETHA, the Honors Program, and the Center for East Texas Studies, and some of the prior arrangements we had enjoyed in past administrations began to change. As a result, the timing seemed right to start thinking about retirement, so there were countless negotiations to that effect, even though it would be a few years before that would be finalized, and in the meantime I continued to run the association. Although I had had open-heart surgery back in 2001, I had fully recovered and still enjoyed what I was doing. Yet I agreed to step aside at some point, and eventually a search committee picked Scott Sosebee, a Texas Tech doctorate, as my successor. What impressed me about Scott out of all the people we interviewed was that he really wanted to be here. He reminds me of the actor John Goodman in stature and attitude, and maybe what associates that is that Goodman played Babe Ruth in a movie, and Scott is a baseball man. He played professionally a little bit and also played in college. Anyway, he is just that kind of boisterous and outgoing guy, and I just love him; he's wonderful. I could not have found a more generous successor than Scott has been. Unfortunately, there was no real training period for him, but most fortunately he has involved me from the day he got here. I was determined not to get in the way of the successor, but he would not let me go, so I agreed to help where I could. At the same time, though, I went to the university president, Baker Pattillo—a close friend—and told him I was not ready to leave the university, and he said, "Well, I'm not ready for you to go either. What would you do?" Coincidentally, Judy had been on an advisory board with Bob Bolen, who was a former mayor of Fort Worth and a special assistant to the chancellor of TCU. He had talked to her at their luncheons and meetings about what he did for his university, so Judy suggested I call Bob Bolen and talk with him about his responsibilities. Her reasoning was that I was involved in a variety of projects, active in the community, a member of the Rotary Club, on the hospital board, and also a member of the Booster Club, which is the oldest men's civic organization in town, so I had connections that could help SFA. So she let him know I wanted to visit with him, and he called me one night and we must have talked on the phone for about an hour about what he does at TCU. Essentially, his job was to do whatever the chancellor wanted him to do. He didn't teach classes, but his value came in the contacts he had throughout the state, including political circles through his mayoral work. He had an extraordinarily valuable Rolodex. Part of his assignment was that he got speakers for the business school, and that could include the CEO of General Motors and other similarly distinguished individuals. So at the end of the call, he said, "Why don't you come up for lunch and I'll get together some of the other guys in the area that do what I do?" And so he did. I went up with a guy named Andy Kesling, who was our information director, because budget-wise, I would have been under his oversight. The good thing for me was that Andy had been at TCU before coming to SFA, so he knew the folks there. We met Bob Bolen, and we met a guy who worked for the Tarrant County Community College system, and a guy who worked for the University of North Texas in the Dallas–Fort Worth area. They were all special assistants to their presidents, and they all three did different things. The key, in other words, was that they did whatever the presidents wanted them to do. So when we came back, Andy put the word in for me and came up with the plan. I first worked on the proposal with interim provost Marlin Young, who was a good friend, and then later the new provost, Richard "Ric" Berry. I had known Ric since he was a student. I directed his mother's thesis, so I knew her, as well as Ric's father. So he just made the new position a reality; this was something Baker said to do, so he did it. He put me in his office, so I report to the provost, not directly to the president, although the president calls when he wants me to do something. I report some of my activities to him, but informally. My formal reporting is always to Berry, and budget-wise I am quartered in the provost office, which is appropriate since I teach a large history survey course every semester. While I enjoyed the change in work, I must confess that I still missed the association, where I had been for thirty-seven years. I liked the associational work, although there were moments of displeasure at times, but when I added it all up it was a good experience for me. Now when I say it was hard to leave, there were never any feelings that my successor would not do well; that never crossed my mind. The worst thing I did to him was to take Portia with me as my new secretary, at least part time. She had to take on other duties as well, but that was her decision to make.

My last official assignment for the association was to speak at the spring 2008 meeting in Tyler. In a way, it was my valedictory address. It was not as difficult an assignment as one might expect; everyone was so good to me, saying nice things and giving me gifts. I was prepared for the speech; it was showtime, so I showed up and I executed. Besides, I was excited about my new job—a new career in my seventies. Not many folks can say that.

So, after all these reminiscences through oral history covering a lifetime of work, here are my closing thoughts on the state of the association. I want it to expand its membership, and particularly to increase the number of younger people, because they become older someday. Both Scott Sosebee and Mark Barringer have been good about that. I don't want the association ever to lose its regional consciousness and sense of place and purpose. There is a place for TSHA, but it is already taken. We need to be the best we can be in this particular region. As for my legacy, I just want everybody to think I did my best. That's it. I did my best.

Epilogue

The first of the oral history interview sessions that formed the core of this memoir got under way in Archie McDonald's office on the morning of Tuesday, March 22, 2011. It began innocently enough, with two old friends—mentor and mentee—talking about what constitutes the boundaries, both geographically and historically, of East Texas. By the time the last session concluded on Thursday, May 26, of that year, we had six digital recordings that varied in length from about an hour to two hours. We had what we thought was a good summation of an honored career that spanned several generations and included countless individuals who shared a common appreciation for Lone Star history.

Within the year that followed, much changed with regard to that story as Archie valiantly waged war against the disease that would eventually prevail and close out the final chapter. Despite the intense pain that became part of his daily existence well into the following year, Archie never gave up hope, and part of that hope was the book you see before you. He did not want to leave until he knew his record was complete. To that end, when he quietly passed away on August 16, 2012, part of the edited manuscript lay on the table beside his bed in the Nacogdoches Medical Center. Memorials and words of praise for the good man's life came quickly and were widespread as countless friends and colleagues struggled to cope with the loss. One of the most heartfelt of remembrances came from his longtime partner in history and folklore, Dr. Francis "Ab" Abernethy—another giant among the chroniclers of Texas who, sadly, is also now departed. Writing in the *Nacogdoches Sentinel*, Abernethy recalled, "Archie was a picky eater, a Yaller Dog Democrat, and a Hardshell Baptist, but we always and often enjoyed each other's company and conversation. I never ceased to admire his energy and his commitment to his discipline. I never ceased to admire his courage and vision. Archie was a true scholar. He searched for knowledge to share, never to hoard. Our loss! Arch was a good buddy. The day of his death was a dark, cold day."

There are myriad lessons to be gleaned from the memoirs of Dr. Archie P. McDonald, but one closing thought he might have wanted to provide the reader is the value of preserving history for the future. He never gave up on that task, and that same stubbornness and perseverance that marked his research and that guided his goal in life came to bear when he sat down to record some of his thoughts to share with others. He clearly understood the value of oral history. Even though he was not a practitioner of the methodology per se, instead pursuing elements of a much more distant past, he always appreciated good stories from remembered history—especially those he remembered himself. It is important to note, then, that there are others out there who have important parts of our past to share but who have not yet been asked to do so. Maybe this book will somehow serve as a reminder that there is still work to be done in Archie's memory. That alone is a legacy worth remembering.

Select Bibliography of Archie P. McDonald Works

AUTHORED BOOKS

The Amazing Grace Baptist Church: Four Decades of Service at Austin Heights. Nacogdoches, TX: Austin Heights Baptist Church, 2007.

Arthur Temple College of Forestry: The Story of Forestry at SFA. Nacogdoches, TX: Stephen F. Austin State University College of Forestry, 2005.

Back Then: Simple Pleasures and Everyday Heroes. Abilene, TX: State House Press, 2005.

Back Then Again: More Simple Pleasures and Everyday Heroes. Nacogdoches, TX: Stephen F. Austin State University Press, 2010.

By Early Candlelight: The Story of Old Milam. Fort Worth, TX: Masonic Home Press, 1967. Reprint, 2007.

Historic Smith County: An Illustrated History of Tyler and Smith County. San Antonio: Historical Publishing Network, Lammert Publications, 2006.

Historic Texas: An Illustrated Chronicle of Texas' Past. San Antonio: For Preservation Texas, Lammert Publications, 1996.

The Lone Star Brand: Products That Make Profits for Others, 1930–2005. Nacogdoches: Kline Printing for Texas Farm Products, 2005.

Nacogdoches. With James G. Partin, Joe Ericson, and Carolyn Ericson. Lufkin, TX: Best of East Texas Publishers, 1995. 2nd ed., 2006.

Nacogdoches. Images of America series. With Hardy Meredith. Charleston, SC: Arcadia Publishing, 2009.

Nacogdoches, Texas—A Pictorial History. With R. G. Dean and Ouida Whitaker Dean. Virginia Beach, VA: Donning, 1996. 2nd ed., 2007.

Pioneers, Poke Sallet and Politics: Vignettes of East Texas Life, History and Folklore. With Bob Bowman. Lufkin, TX: Best of East Texas Publishers, 2001.

Stephen F. Austin State University Jacks: Images of Sports. With Hardy Meredith. Charleston, SC: Arcadia Publishing, 2009.

Texas: A Compact History. Abilene, TX: State House Press, 2007.

Texas: All Hail the Mighty State. Austin: Eakin Press, 1983. Rev. ed., 1991.

"Texas: A Sesquicentennial Presentation." *Dallas Times-Herald*, March 7, 1982.

Texas: What Do You Know about the Lone Star State? Fort Worth: Texas Christian University Press, 1993.

Texas: Yesterday and Today. With Gary S. Elbow, Mary Garcia Metzger, and Rodolfo Rocha. Fourth-grade text. Morristown, NJ: Silver Burdett, 1988. Rev. ed., 1996.

Travis. Austin: Pemberton Press, 1977. Reprint, Eakin Press, 1990.

"Uncommon Valor . . . Common Virtue": A Tribute to Bennett P. Blake, U.S. Marine on Iwo Jima. Compiled by Roy M. Blake and Archie P. McDonald. Lufkin, TX: Best of East Texas Publishers, 1999.

Water, Rails, and Oil: South Jefferson County. San Antonio: Historical Publishing Network, Lammert Publications, 2008.

Where the Corn Grows Tall. Austin: Eakin Press, 1991.

EDITED BOOKS

Blacks in East Texas History. Edited with Bruce A. Glasrud. College Station: Texas A&M University Press, 2008.

Dare-Devils All: Texas Mier Expedition, 1842–1844. By J. M. Nance. Austin: Eakin Press, 1998.

Dare-Devils All. Vol. II, *Biographical Data on 152 Members of the Mier Expedition.* By J. M. Nance. Austin: Eakin Press, 2002.

Eastern Texas History. Austin: Pemberton Press, 1978.

Encyclopedia USA. Open-ended encyclopedia published at the rate of two or three volumes per year, for Academic International Press. Vols. 4–12.

Fighting Men: The Western Military Heritage. Dubuque, IA: Kendall-Hunt, 1970.

First United Methodist Church, San Augustine, Texas 1837–1976. Wolfe City, TX: Henington Publishing, 1976.

Helpful Cooking Hints for HouseHusbands of Uppity Women. Dallas: E-Heart Press, 1988. Reprint, University of North Texas Press, 2001.

Hurrah for Texas! The Diary of Adolphus Sterne. Waco: Texian Press, 1969. Reprint, Eakin Press, 1986.

Make Me a Map of the Valley: The Civil War Journal of Stonewall Jackson's Topographer. Dallas: Southern Methodist University Press, 1973; College Station: Texas A&M University Press, 1973.

The Mexican War: Crisis for American Democracy. Boston: D. C. Heath, 1969.

Nacogdoches: Wilderness Outpost to Modern City, 1779–1979. Nacogdoches: Texas Committee for the Humanities (Grant Report), 1979.

A Nation of Sovereign States: Secession & War in the Confederacy. Journal of Confederate History Series, vol. 10. Murfreesboro, TN: Southern Heritage Press, 1994.

Notable East Texans. Austin: Eakin Press, 1986.

On This Day of New Beginnings: Selected Inaugural Addresses of Texas Governors. Austin: Texas State Library, 1979.

Recollections of a Long Life. Nashville: Blue-Gray Press, 1974.

Shooting Stars: Heroes and Heroines of Western Film. Bloomington: Indiana University Press, 1987.

The Texas Experience. College Station: Texas A&M University Press, 1986.

The Texas Heritage. With Ben H. Procter. St. Louis: Forum Press, 1980. 3rd and 4th eds., Harlan Davidson, 1998 and 2003.

"To Live and Die in Dixie": How the South Formed a Nation. Journal of Confederate History Series, vol. 20. Murfreesboro, TN: Southern Heritage Press, 1999.

What Makes East Texas, East Texas. Edited with Bruce A. Glasrud. Nacogdoches: East Texas Historical Association, 2009.

MONOGRAPHS

Americans Elect Their President from Washington to Reagan or Mondale? Published serially in the *Nacogdoches Sunday Sentinel*, September 2 through November 11, 1984.

America to 1877 Study Guide. St. Louis: River City Publishers, 1983.

History of the School of Forestry. Nacogdoches, TX: Stephen F. Austin State University, 2005.

History of Texas Farm Products. Nacogdoches, TX: Locally published, 2005.

Hotel Fredonia: "For the Convenience of Travelers and Guests." Nacogdoches, TX: Story-Wright for the Fredonia Hotel Corporation, 2005.

The Old Stone Fort. Austin: Texas State Historical Association, 1981.

Sentinel of Service. Nacogdoches, TX: Stone Fort National Bank, 2003.

The Texas Republic. Boston: American Book Company, 1981.

The Trail to San Jacinto. Boston: American Book Company, 1982.

Travis: One Chief Rol'd among the Rest. Victoria, TX: Victoria College, 1986.

Index

CPSIA information can be obtained
at www.ICGtesting.com
Printed in the USA
LVOW04s2102080716
495556LV00005B/7/P